AS/A-LEVEL YEAR 1
STUDENT GUIDE

AQA

Politics

Politics of the UK

Nick Gallop

Series editor: Eric Magee

HODDER
EDUCATION
AN HACHETTE UK COMPANY

Hodder Education, an Hachette UK company, Blenheim Court, George Street, Banbury, Oxfordshire OX16 5BH

Orders

Bookpoint Ltd, 130 Park Drive, Milton Park, Abingdon, Oxfordshire OX14 4SB

tel: 01235 827720

fax: 01235 400401

e-mail: education@bookpoint.co.uk

Lines are open 9.00 a.m.–5.00 p.m., Monday to Saturday, with a 24-hour message answering service. You can also order through the Hodder Education website: www.hoddereducation.co.uk

© Nick Gallop 2017

ISBN 978-1-4718-9317-9

First printed 2017

Impression number 5 4 3 2

Year 2021 2020 2019 2018

This Guide has been written specifically to support students preparing for the AQA AS and A-level Politics examinations. The content has been neither approved nor endorsed by AQA and remains the sole responsibility of the author.

Cover photograph: sibgat/123RF

Typeset by Integra Software Services Pvt. Ltd., Pondicherry, India

Printed in Dubai

Hachette UK's policy is to use papers that are natural, renewable and recyclable products and made from wood grown in sustainable forests. The logging and manufacturing processes are expected to conform to the environmental regulations of the country of origin.

Contents

■ Getting the most from this book

Exam tips

Advice on key points in the text to help you learn and recall content, avoid pitfalls, and polish your exam technique in order to boost your grade.

Knowledge check

Rapid-fire questions throughout the Content Guidance section to check your understanding.

Knowledge check answers

1 Turn to the back of the book for the Knowledge check answers.

Summaries

■ Each core topic is rounded off by a bullet-list summary for quick-check reference of what you need to know.

Exam-style questions

Commentary on the questions

Tips on what you need to do to gain full marks, indicated by the icon ⓔ

Sample student answers

Practise the questions, then look at the student answers that follow.

Questions & Answers

■ 6-mark questions (AS only)

There are four of these questions on the AS paper which are assessed using AO1 only.

What do you need to do?
■ Provide a clear and accurate definition of the concept, term or phrase identified in the question.
■ Develop your explanation and demonstrate your deeper understanding by selecting and using appropriate examples in support of your answer.

Democracy and participation

Explain, with examples, the concept of direct democracy.   [6 marks]

ⓔ You should ensure that you have provided a clear and accurate definition of the term direct democracy, along with supporting examples that demonstrate what this means in practice. High-level responses will also demonstrate conceptual understanding of the difference between direct democracy and representative democracy and be able to provide examples from states other than the UK (e.g. Switzerland and the USA).

Student answer

Direct democracy is a process of decision making whereby the people make important political and constitutional decisions, not their representatives. The term originated in ancient Athens when citizens of the city-state (which only included free men) had the opportunity to debate and vote on policy. The practical considerations of mass participation in multiple decisions mean that direct democracy is not possible in modern democratic states and the UK is principally a representative democracy in which elections are used to transfer the responsibility for voting and debating to elected officials. However, there are some states that do use direct democracy frequently. Switzerland has around a dozen direct decision-making opportunities each year on a whole range of civic matters, and California sees multiple questions on the ballot — from outlawing capital punishment to legalising marijuana. In the UK, opportunities for direct decision making on the part of the people are far less frequent. In fact, up until 20 years ago, they were considered (by Clement Attlee) to be 'alien to our traditions'. Since 1997 however some of the most significant constitutional changes have been determined by popular referendum — from the creation of devolved assemblies in Scotland and Wales (1997) to retaining the Westminster electoral system (2011) to Scotland saying 'No' to independence (2014) and the decision to leave the EU (2016).

ⓔ 6/6 marks awarded (Level 3). This answer provides a clear definition with a brief comparison to representative democracy. Although the examples could focus on the UK prior to other areas of the world first, the range and scope of the student's response is very strong.

72   AQA Politics

Commentary on sample student answers

Read the comments (preceded by the icon ⓔ) showing how many marks each answer would be awarded in the exam and exactly where marks are gained or lost.

■About this book

The aim of this Student Guide is to prepare you for the 'Politics of the UK' section of AQA AS Paper 1 Government and Politics of the UK and AQA A-level Paper 1 Government and Politics of the UK.

■ For AS students, the topics covered in this guide comprise half of the topics required for the examination on Government and Politics of the UK — they appear in the specification under the heading 'Politics of the UK'.

■ For A-level students, the topics covered in this guide form half of Paper 1 Government and Politics of the UK. A-level Politics Paper 1 represents a third of the papers required to complete the A-level examination.

In both cases, all of the topics could be examined in the exam. It is therefore vital that you are familiar and confident with all the material.

The **Content Guidance** section covers all the topics largely in the order that they appear on the AQA AS and A-level specifications. You are strongly advised to have a copy of the most recent version of the specification to refer to as you go through the topics. For the section on the 'Politics of the UK' there are five main topics:

■ Democracy and participation
■ Elections and referendums
■ Political parties
■ Pressure groups
■ The European Union

You should use the Content Guidance to ensure that you are familiar with all the key concepts and terms, statistics, issues and arguments, and have a range of relevant examples you can quote in your answers because you are aware of the relative significance of these principles and concepts.

The **Questions & Answers** section provides an opportunity for you to hone your exam technique and to become familiar with the skills and structures that examiners are looking for in the AS and A-level exams. It is not possible to provide sample questions and answers for each section of the exam on every topic, so you need to be aware that any parts of the specification could be tested in any sections of the examination.

This guide does not provide a complete range of examples or go into full detail, so you should use it alongside other resources such as class notes and articles in *Politics Review* (published by Hodder Education). You should also use websites such as the BBC, TotalPolitics.com, The Guardian, The Times Red Box and www.politics.co.uk to keep up to date with current news.

Content Guidance

■Democracy and participation

The nature of democracy

Democracy provides the basis for any modern state that claims to support ideals such as justice, equality and government by consent. It is a concept that has been in existence — in various forms — for many thousands of years and yet remains as contested and as disputed as ever. Central to any conceptual or practical understanding of democracy are *people*, and the extent to which they are able to influence the decision-making process within a state. In addition to this, key components of democracy include:

- frequent, free and fair elections to provide **legitimacy** for the government and its activities
- the tolerance of different opinions, viewpoints, parties and political groups and an independent media
- protection of the rights of citizens
- government that is accountable to the people, that rules according to clearly understood limits on its power, under a constitution and with an independent judiciary

The functions of democracy, the different types of democracy and an evaluation of the nature of democracy in the UK are all discussed later in this topic. But the initial focus is on the extent to which the people in the UK have been able to exercise the most fundamental act within any democratic system — that of voting.

Suffrage in the UK: debates and issues

How suffrage has changed since the Great Reform Act (1832) to the present

Britain may well be considered one of the world's oldest and most enduring democracies, but the historical basis for its democracy is far from strong. For many centuries prior to 1832 only a tiny fraction of the population voted for the individuals who represented them. Indeed the selection of the UK's representative assembly lay in the hands of a very few, being the preserve of a wealthy, male, land-owning elite.

While the **franchise** has been extended significantly since then, the process to gain the right to vote has been a long and arduous one for many groups within society. In the UK today all citizens over the age of 18 are allowed to vote in public, political elections, with the exception of only a small number of individuals. This entitlement is known as **universal suffrage**, is granted to 71.5% of the population and is protected by law.

Democracy The word comes from two Greek words —*demos* (people) and *kratia* (rule) meaning the people rule.

Legitimacy Elections provide governments with the right to govern by the consent of the people.

Exam tip

The UK's democracy is often prefixed by a number of important terms, each stressing slightly different aspects of it. It is referred to as a representative democracy, a liberal democracy and a pluralist democracy.

Franchise The franchise is the right to vote in public political elections.

Universal suffrage Term given to every adult within a state having the right to vote.

Even so, areas of contention still remain:

- Should 16- and 17-year-olds be permitted to vote, as they were in the Scottish independence referendum in 2014?
- Should adults continue to exercise their right to vote despite being in prison?

The extension of the franchise

The extension of the franchise in the UK began in the early part of the nineteenth century. The Representation of the People Act 1832, known widely as the Great Reform Act, was in its own words enacted to 'take effectual Measures for correcting divers Abuses that have long prevailed in the Choice of Members to serve in the Commons House of Parliament'. Such 'abuses' took many forms:

- Elections took place in 'boroughs' — the number of electors within them ranging from under 10 (these were known as 'rotten boroughs') to over 12,000.
- Some boroughs were controlled by powerful local aristocrats — the Duke of Norfolk controlled the selection of MPs in up to 11 boroughs for many decades.
- The qualifications required to be entitled to vote varied widely from one region to another, though less than 4% of the total population were eligible.

The most significant changes brought in by the Great Reform Act were to:

- extend the franchise to around 800,000 people, or 1 in 5 male adults and around 6% of the total population
- create seats in the House of Commons to represent the cities that had begun to spring up as the Industrial Revolution gathered pace
- disband many rotten boroughs by redrawing constituency boundaries

In fact, the Great Reform Act was to be the first of many legislative acts over 150 years that would see the franchise gradually extended to all adults (see Table 1)

Table 1 The extension of the franchise in the UK

Year	How the franchise was extended
1832	The Great Reform Act extended the right to vote to male property owners (1 in 5 men).
1867	The Second Reform Act saw voting rights extended to skilled male workers (1 in 3 men).
1887	The Third Reform Act extendd the vote to all working men (2 in 3 men).
1918	The Representation of the People Act extended voting rights to all men over 21 and to women over 30.
1928	Voting rights were extended to all women over 21.
1969	Voting rights were extended to everyone aged 18 or above.

Debates regarding gender, class, ethnicity and age

Women and the right to vote

The Representation of the People Act 1918 made women eligible to vote in UK-wide elections for the first time. The Act enfranchised women over the age of 30, as well as all men over the age of 21. The franchise was extended 10 years later to include all women over 21.

Knowledge check 1

Explain briefly which adults are **ineligible** to vote in elections in the UK.

Exam tip

As you progress through your course remember that you will get credit for using subject-specific vocabulary. Consider creating and learning your own glossary of key political terms and concepts.

The 1918 Act came at a time of significant social and political change for women. The workplace was transforming, with the availability of clerical jobs and some professional careers — such as in healthcare and education — for the first time. But even in 1918 there remained much debate about whether women should be enfranchised. At the time, arguments that women should *not* be given the right to vote included:

- Many women did not want the right to vote, preferring to be represented in matters of national politics by their husbands or fathers.
- Men and women played very different roles in society, evidenced by the fact that women had not fought to defend their country in the First World War.
- The system 'worked': men were seen to have more interest and engagement with national issues while women focused on local affairs.

However, the more enlightened members of society in the early 1900s argued conversely that:

- Denying women the right to vote undermined any claim that Britain had to be a democratic state.
- Women were perfectly capable of performing what had traditionally been seen as men's roles, evidenced by their impact and sacrifices on the home front during the war.
- Voting should be considered a fundamental right — not restricted on the basis of gender, wealth or any other social subdivision.

The Representation of the People Act 1928 secured parity between the genders with all women over the age of 21 gaining the right to vote. The final 1969 Act was an acknowledgement that social changes made the minimum voting age appear antiquated to even the most conservative of onlookers. With 18-year-olds better educated, better informed and more socially and economically independent than at any previous time, Parliament passed the Act to remove the final barrier to universal adult suffrage.

The suffragists and suffragettes

The enfranchisement of women is inextricably linked to the activities of two highly prominent campaign groups — the **suffragists** and the **suffragettes**. Over 50 years before the 1918 Reform Act, Parliament was presented with a petition to grant the right to vote to women. The failure of this 1866 petition led to the formation of groups committed to women's suffrage in all regions of the UK over the following decades. The movement took on a more coherent and organised character in the wake of New Zealand granting the right to vote for women in 1893. In 1897 **Millicent Fawcett** founded the National Union of Women's Suffrage Societies (NUWSS), also known as the suffragists.

Characterised by their restrained activities consisting largely of letter writing, educational meetings and peaceful marches, the suffragists edged the cause of women's suffrage up the political agenda, claiming more than 100,000 members by 1914. But this process was all too slow for some activists. In 1903 Emmeline Pankhurst and her daughters Christabel and Sylvia set up a splinter group, the Women's Social and Political Union (WSPU) known widely as the suffragettes. In direct contrast to the

Knowledge check 2

Explain why the First World War was considered a major 'catalyst' for women's enfranchisement.

Suffragists A general term for the members of the suffrage movement, particularly relating to the NUWSS.

Suffragettes The more militant members of the WSPU, formed in 1903, who advocated 'deeds not words'.

Millicent Fawcett Feminist, campaigner and president of the National Union of Women's Suffrage Societies (NUWSS). The Fawcett Society remains a charity campaigning for women's equal rights.

suffragists, the suffragettes' slogan of 'deeds not words' saw the arrival of more militant tactics involving civil disobedience, vandalism, arson and hunger strikes.

Would women have been granted the right to vote without the militant tactics of the suffragettes?

No:

- Within 15 years of the foundation of the suffragettes, the 1918 Reform Act was passed — testament to the newly assertive campaigning of the group.
- The step-change in tactics and level of commitment from women who would stop at nothing — including sacrificing their own lives — was a defining moment in the movement.

Yes:

- The suffragettes' violent tactics were suspended during the First World War — and the 1918 Reform Act was a direct reaction to women's roles during the war years.
- The level of violence was seen as irresponsible and reckless by many men and women — the suffragettes saw their membership dwindle from 1913 onwards.

Gender: issues and electoral participation

Since the 1969 Reform Act, analysts of voting behaviour have seen discernible differences in the way that men and women cast their votes — a feature often referred to as the **gender gap**. While many refute the notion that women's complex political preferences can be lumped together, in recent elections there has been a disparity between the genders:

- In the 2010 general election women's turnout was 4% lower than that of men. It was widely reported than more than 9 million women failed to vote in 2010, compared to 8 million men.
- In the 2015 general election there was a distinct gender-based difference in party support. In an election won by the Conservatives, Labour enjoyed a 6% lead among women under 50.
- In the 2017 general election there was only a small gender gap between men and women, while women were equally split between Labour and the Conservatives (43% to 43%), men supported the Conservatives more than women by 45% to 39%.

It was long held to be true that from a voting perspective, women were more conformist, more family-orientated and therefore more likely to identify with the Conservative Party — something borne out by immediate postwar election data. In the decades up to 2010, however, the changing role of women in society and the Labour Party's courting of the female vote (seen clearly in the 101 female Labour MPs elected in 1997) led to a reversal of the gender gap and a greater proportion of women voting for the Labour Party.

More recently, however, the notion of a 'gender gap' — and the belief that there are distinct women's issues — was challenged. Jeremy Corbyn was branded 'patronising' for suggesting that childcare was the number one priority for women. The Labour Party policy to extend nursery vouchers is 'not just a women's issue' and 'the women's vote is largely a myth…the economy is the top issue for both men and women' said BBC *Woman's Hour* presenter Emma Barnett in May 2017.

Gender gap A term that usually refers to well-established differences in voting turnout and patterns based on gender.

In the 2017 general election, the number of female representatives reached a peak with 208 women in the Commons, up from 191 in 2015. Overall, in 2017 32% of MPs were women, but there are significant variations between parties: for Labour the figure was 45%, for the Conservatives 21%.

Enfranchising the working classes

The earliest major movements towards universal suffrage were not based on gender but on *class*. In perspective, the 'Great' Reform Act of 1832 was more of an administrative exercise, mainly reforming constituency boundaries and barely bringing 2% more men to the polls. The Representation of the People Act 1867 (the Second Reform Act) on the other hand was a major move to enfranchise the urban male working classes and was the product of a significant shift in thinking about citizenship, democracy and rights over the intervening decades:

- The **Chartist** movement was a major working-class movement between 1838 and 1857, based primarily in the industrial north. Mass meetings, petitions signed by millions of working men, and some revolutionary insurrections in South Wales and Yorkshire characterised a movement that put universal male suffrage, the **secret ballot**, and other social reforms at the top of the political agenda.
- The Reform League was established in 1865 to campaign for universal male suffrage. It gathered many leading figures from international working men's movements, organised demonstrations and campaigned successfully for the Reform Act of 1867. The group was formally dissolved in 1869.
- The American Civil War had come to symbolise enfranchisement, citizenship and progressive democratic ideals against the dictatorial establishment of the Southern States. The Union victory in 1865 further emboldened liberalising forces in Britain.

It took 50 years — the time between the Second and Fourth Reform Acts (1918) — for all men over the age of 21 to be granted the right to vote.

Social class: issues and electoral participation

Class refers to the hierarchical arrangement of socioeconomic groups made up of people who share similar jobs and income, wealth and outlook. The widely-used quote from political historian Peter Pulzer in 1967 that 'class is the basis of British party politics, all else is embellishment and detail' underlines the significance of the link between class and electoral participation. In terms of understanding this link:

- **Sociological theories** of voting behaviour emphasise the importance of upbringing and family in embedding strong support for a 'natural' party. (In 1964 the number of *very strong* party supporters was measured at 44%.)
- **Class identification** reflects the common bonds felt to exist between those with shared socioeconomic characteristics — bonds highly likely to shape cultural and political outlook.
- **Party alignment** (or **partisan alignment**) stresses the strong relationships that exist between the two main parties and the classes that they were perceived to represent — the Labour Party and the working class, and the Conservative Party and the middle and upper classes. In 1966, 67% of voters were classified as 'class voters' — supporters of the 'natural' party of their class interests.

> **Knowledge check 3**
> Identify two reasons why the gender gap has closed in recent decades.

> **Chartists** A national protest movement in the mid-1800s that focused on democratic reforms for an industrialised society, taking its name from the six points within the People's Charter of 1838.

> **Secret ballot** The protection of electors from the consequences of their vote was enshrined in the Ballot Act 1872.

> **Partisan alignment** An enduring association between a group of people and a particular political party meaning that the outlook and views of the group and the party become 'aligned'.

However, the strong links felt to exist between class, party and voting behaviour had declined by the start of the twenty-first century (see Table 2).

- In the 1959 general election 62% of working-class voters supported the Labour Party — this had fallen to 38% by 1983.
- Many traditional middle-class voters supported Tony Blair and New Labour in 1997 (and again in 2001) — they were largely responsible for the 10% swing to the Labour Party.
- In 2005 just 9% of voters expressed *very strong* support for either of the two main parties.

Table 2 Voters supporting their 'natural class' (%)

Year	% of voters supporting their 'natural class'
1979	51
1987	44
2010	38

Two explanations for the shifting links between class, party and voting behaviour are particularly relevant:

- **Dealignment** explains the weakening links between parties and their traditional class-based supporters as a consequence of changing socioeconomic forces.
- **Embourgeoisement** refers to an expansion in the number of people who consider themselves to be 'middle class'. While this is partly explained by changing employment trends it is also a result of deliberate attempts by political parties to broaden their appeal.

In 2017, YouGov's post-election analysis revealed that 'the class divide in British politics seems to have closed and it is no longer a very good indicator of voting intention'. Labour remains ahead among voters from semi-skilled and unskilled manual occupations, unemployed people and those in the lowest grade occupations — but only by 3 percentage points (44% to 41%).

Ethnicity: issues and electoral participation

In 1950, the number of black, Asian and minority ethnic (BAME) people in the UK was less than 100,000 and mainly confined to dockland areas such as London, Liverpool, Cardiff and Bristol: small communities close to the original arrival point of many immigrants. Postwar immigrants were mostly of Caribbean origin, but since then, immigration patterns have changed significantly — and even more so very recently. The non-white population grew from 6.6 million in 2001 to 9.1 million in 2011 according to the most recent UK census. In 2017, just over 13% of the UK population was estimated to be 'non-white' with predictions that this will rise to a third by 2050.

While BAME groups in Britain have not been subject to the same levels of state-sponsored disenfranchisement seen in the southern states of the USA, electoral participation among BAME groups has traditionally been significantly lower than the national average. Within many BAME communities, views that mainstream politics under-represents and marginalises them are widely-held and have led to

Exam tip

Terms like 'old working class' and 'new working class' are helpful to demonstrate your knowledge of how class and voting has changed.

deep-seated feelings of cynicism towards British democracy. Consciously opting out was seen by many as the only valid form of political expression.

> ## Synoptic link
>
> ### Race and voting in the USA
>
> Segregation continued to exist in many southern states of the USA after the Civil War in spite of several constitutional amendments making it illegal to discriminate on the grounds of race. In defiance of these, southern states passed legislation and constitutional changes at state level, which required potential voters to pass literacy tests or pay a poll tax in order to register to vote. These deliberately affected vast numbers of impoverished African Americans, many of whom had only recently been freed from slavery. Such practices continued until the passing of the 24th Amendment to the United States Constitution in 1964 and the 1965 Voting Rights Act which prohibited their use.

In 1996, Operation Black Vote (OBV) was founded to encourage black and Asian voters to register and participate. OBV runs imaginative campaigns, particularly in the run-up to general elections. Twenty years on, in 2015, black celebrities painted their faces white and appeared in advertisements alongside the OBV slogan 'If you don't register to vote, you are taking the colour out of Britain'.

Statistically, ethnic minority voters have tended to live in less affluent, urban communities and have disproportionately supported the Labour Party whose policies are seen as more sympathetic towards them. In 2010, 16% of ethnic minority voters supported the Conservative Party compared to 68% supporting the Labour Party (this compares to 31% of white voters who supported the Labour Party).

Following the 2015 general election though, a report by think tank British Future showed that 33% of BAME voters supported the Conservatives, a new record for the party which had previously struggled to appeal to this group of voters. For the Labour Party, the high concentration of BAME supporters in a small number of constituencies means that their strength of support is not reflected in a large number of winning seats.

Following the 2017 general election, ten new black and minority ethnic MPs entered the Commons, and there was only one loss — there are now 51 such MPs. According to Operation Black Vote, the significant difference between 2017 and previous elections is that the new MPs are standing and winning in constituencies outside the biggest cities:

- New MPs in 2017 included Preet Gill, the first female Sikh MP, in Birmingham Edgbaston.
- BAME MPs still only make up 7.8% of the new parliament, compared to around 14% of the population as a whole.

Age: issues and electoral participation

There are two main issues relating to age and political/electoral participation:
- Older people vote in disproportionately higher numbers with the effect that political issues and party policies are consistently skewed in their favour.

Knowledge check 4

Explain briefly why concentrated support within BAME communities makes it difficult for Labour to win a 'fair share' of parliamentary seats.

Conversely, the disengagement of 18–35 year-olds has led to their perceived marginalisation by mainstream politics and politicians.

- The age at which people are permitted to vote could be lowered to include 16- and 17-year-olds.

With regard to the first issue, the 2017 general election revealed that age is a new dividing line in British electoral politics. Figure 1 shows party support by age in the June 2017 election and demonstrates the very stark difference between younger and older voters. Among first time voters, Labour was 47 percentage points ahead of the Conservatives, while among over 70s, the Conservatives were 50 percentage points clear of Labour.

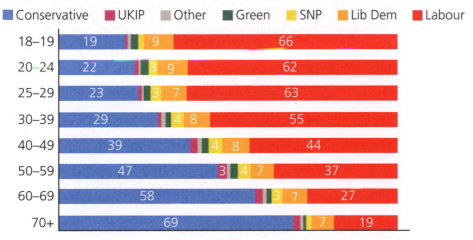

Figure 1 Voting by age in the 2017 election (%)

There are many theories and models about the longstanding support for the Conservative Party among older voters. These are most often based on the following points:

- The kind of policies usually favoured by the Tories — law and order, pro-family, traditional values — tend to be a more natural 'fit' for older votes.
- People become more 'conservative' (in the sense of wanting to preserve institutions and behaviours of their past) and less radical as they grow older.
- Older voters in the 2010s were 'young' voters in the late 1970s and 1980s — when the Conservative Party was popular and voters' political views became embedded. Some predict that older voters in the 2030s will be more inclined to support the Labour Party for similar reasons.

Compounding the issue of party support is the fact that older people turn out to vote in far higher numbers. The age difference in overall turnout is significant and in 2017, young people were less likely to vote than older people: 57% of 18- and 19 year-olds voted compared to 84% of those aged 70+.

Consequently, issues that affect older people — such as pensions, healthcare, non-means-tested benefits (e.g. free bus passes and free TV licences) — are far more likely to be championed or protected by both main parties, but especially by the Conservative Party.

In terms of the second issue, the argument for lowering the voting age to include 16 years old was given a boost by the inclusion of 16- and 17-year-olds in the Scottish independence referendum in 2014. In this referendum, younger voters engaged enthusiastically with the national debate and turned out in large numbers to vote: 89% of 16- and 17-year-olds had registered to vote by the time of the referendum and survey data revealed that over 75% of this age category actually voted, compared to just 54% of 18–24 year olds. The debate over lowering the voting age is summarised below.

Debate over lowering the voting age to 16

The voting age *should* be lowered to include 16- and 17-year-olds:

- In an age of rapid information and communication technology, young people are more engaged and much better informed than previous generations.
- With turnout so low among 18–24-year-olds, engaging voters while they are younger and while still in school or college could support more engaged and responsible patterns of political participation.
- 16-year-olds are old enough to pay taxes, get married and serve in the armed forces — it is difficult to justify why they are not old enough to vote.

The voting age *should not* be lowered to include 16- and 17-year-olds:

- Many people would argue that the vast majority of 16- and 17-year-olds are too young to be able to make rational judgements.
- The current limit to voting at 18 years old is clearly understood and accepted as appropriate by most people. If the voting age is lowered from 18, what is the justification for only including 16- and 17-year-olds and not 14-year-olds or 15-year-olds? Why might 16-year-olds be able to decide on complex political issues in a way that 15-year-olds cannot?
- Very few 16- and 17-year-olds work to an extent that they pay tax. Their stake in society is likely to be low.

> ## Synoptic link
>
> ### Voting ages around the world
> The age at which people are legally entitled to vote varies around the world. The minimum age is 16 in Argentina, Austria, Brazil, Cuba, Ecuador, Nicaragua and the three self-governing British Crown Dependencies: the Isle of Man, Jersey and Guernsey. People aged 16–18 can vote in Bosnia, Serbia and Montenegro if employed. The highest minimum voting age is 21 in several nations.

Suffrage as a human right

The question of whether the right to vote should be considered a '**human right**' is a thought-provoking one. In addition to the debate over lowering the age of voting to 16, this debate is often framed around prisoners' voting rights. Prisoners serving sentence make up the biggest category of disenfranchised UK citizens in public elections.

The Human Rights Act protects our right to free elections, which includes our right to vote. Article 1 Protocol 3 states that the UK will 'hold free elections at reasonable intervals by secret ballot, under conditions which will ensure the free expression of the opinion of the people in the choice of the legislature [Parliament]'.

Human rights These refer to rights inherent to all human beings, regardless of nationality, gender, race, religion or any other status.

However, in one of the most recent test cases determined by the European Court of Human Rights (ECtHR) the right to vote was firmly declared not to be an absolute right, with the court declaring in the case of *Hirst* v *UK* that:

> **the rights bestowed by Article 3 of Protocol No. 1 are not absolute...There are numerous ways of organising and running electoral systems and a wealth of differences...in historical development, cultural diversity and political thought within Europe...it is for each [country]...to mould into their own democratic vision.**

The ruling set out that while the right to vote was not absolute; denying the right to vote is indeed a significant act — one that must be in proportion to the circumstances that require a ban or denial to be put in place. Critics of the ban on prisoners voting maintain that — whatever we feel about the activities of those in jail — it undermines the most basic principles of universal suffrage. The ban does not discriminate according to the severity of the sentence — those serving life sentences for murder are subject to the same 'blanket ban' as those serving a very short sentence for the non-payment of a fine.

Different types of democracy: direct and representative

Direct democracy

The term **direct democracy** refers to systems where people are directly involved in the political decisions that affect them. In modern democratic states where direct democracy is prevalent, it is usually seen in the form of referendums or initiatives. There are some significant arguments for and against the use of direct democracy.

Advantages of direct democracy include:
- It is seen as the 'first best' or purest form of democracy.
- Decisions made by the people can resolve long-standing issues (such as the UK's membership of the EU).
- Decisions receive direct consent from the people — and the resolutions are effectively entrenched.

Disadvantages of direct democracy include:
- The tyranny of the majority – just because 51% of people believe something, it does not mean it is 'right'.
- How educated are the people about complex long- and short-term issues? How open are people to manipulation by powerful groups?
- It undermines the experience and mediating influence of elected officials within a representative democracy.

Representative democracy

Representative democracy refers to political systems in which people hand over their decision-making power to others — usually to people elected into office to perform the vital democratic functions of debating and voting on major political issues. Some

Knowledge check 5

Outline and explain one argument in favour and one argument against prisoners having the right to vote.

Direct democracy A system or situation in which people rather than elected representatives make the decisions that affect them.

Knowledge check 6

Identify two examples of referendums that correspond to an advantage and a disadvantage of direct democracy as listed.

Representative democracy The principle that people are represented in government by elected officials rather than taking part in the decision-making process themselves.

aspects of representative democracy were clearly articulated by Edmund Burke as long ago as 1774. Burke told his Bristol constituents that 'your representative owes you not his industry only but his judgement' and 'he betrays you if he sacrifices it to your opinion'. The Burkean view clearly emphasises that representatives are not delegates but instead are able to make decisions that are contrary to our wishes, with the expectation that they are accountable for them in future elections.

In keeping with direct democracy, there are arguments in favour of and against representative democracy.

Advantages of representative democracy include:

- Elected representatives tend to have expertise and experience that many voters may lack.
- With more regular involvement in the decision-making process, elected representatives may be more likely to consider issues rationally, objectively and with long-term national interests in mind.
- Along with elected office come expectations of responsible behaviour and accountability.

Disadvantages of representative democracy include:

- Elected representatives may be swayed in their decision-making by party loyalty or other allegiances.
- Elected representatives may place personal, subjective views over the effective representation of their constituents.
- Representative democracy is only as good as the mechanism that turns votes into seats. Under some electoral systems, basic expectations of fair representation are not met.

What are the problems with the UK's representative democracy?

The UK's democracy has a number of features that are prerequisites for well-functioning representative democracies. These include regular elections to elect representatives at several levels of government, various ways to engage formally with the democratic process — through party or union membership for example — and a range of other more informal ways to express views, participate or hold a government to account.

However, there are also significant areas of weakness within the UK's representative democracy, highlighted by reformers and critics alike. Criticisms include:

- General elections do not produce accurate translations of votes to seats: the lack of proportionality of the voting system used to elect MPs to Parliament produces majority party governments based on minorities of support. In 2015, the Conservative government received just 38% of the votes cast.
- The uncodified constitutional arrangements do not adequately check the power of the executive and a lack of separation of powers between branches of government is exploited by a dominant, yet unrepresentative, executive branch.
- A major element of the UK's legislative body is unelected. The House of Lords is mostly appointed.

Exam tip

Make sure all your responses on aspects of democracy — whether direct or representative — are supported by examples. Further examples of referendums can be found in the next section.

Patterns of participation and different forms of participation

Significant changes over recent decades in the way that people participate in politics are not difficult to identify. While the changing shape of political participation is complex — and subject to regional and demographic variations — the transition is often regarded as a decline in conventional (or traditional) forms of participation countered by a rise in unconventional participation.

The decline in 'conventional' participation

Conventional participation refers to ways of engaging with the political process that have been around for some time and which are seen as being more 'traditional', such as voting in elections and referendums and joining a political party or a union. Significant examples of conventional participation declining include:

- **Turnout** in postwar general elections averaged over 75%, but fell to an average of below 62% for the three general elections between 2001 and 2010 (see Table 3). While turnout for the two most recent referendums was relatively high — 84.6% in the Scottish independence referendum in 2014 and 72.2% in the EU referendum in 2016 — the UK-wide AV referendum in 2011 saw a turnout of just 42.2%.
- **Party membership** has seen a very significant decline in the decades since the Second World War. The Conservative Party's 2.8 million members in the mid-1950s had fallen to below 150,000 by 2013. Labour Party membership fell to below 200,000 in 2010 but by March 2017, prompted by recent leadership elections and challenges, it had risen to around 517,000 members.
- **Union membership** fell from its 13 million peak in the late 1970s to just over half that (7.01 million) in 2014. Figures from the Department for Business Innovation and Skills indicated that up to 2009 union membership was falling by around 165,000 members each year. Since then, and in the 5 years between 2009 and 2014, figures from the Office of National Statistics put the total decline in union membership at just under 320,000, averaging a drop-off rate of over 60,000 members per year.

Latest party membership figures

According to the latest available estimates from political parties' head offices, press releases and media estimates:

- The **Labour Party** had around 517,000 members, as of March 2017.
- The **Conservative Party** had 149,800 members as of December 2013, the latest available estimate published by CCHQ.
- The **Scottish National Party** had around 120,000 members, as of July 2016.
- The **Liberal Democrat Party** had 82,000 members, as of February 2017.
- The **Green Party** (England and Wales) has 55,500 members, as of July 2016.
- **UKIP** had around 39,000 members, as of July 2016.
- The **Plaid Cymru** had 8,273 members, as of July 2016.

Source: www.parliament.gov

Turnout The percentage of registered voters who cast a vote at an election.

Table 3 Turnout at UK general elections

Year	Turnout (%)
1950	83.9
1964	77.1
1979	76.0
1992	77.7
1997	71.4
2001	59.4
2005	61.4
2010	65.1
2015	66.1
2017	68.7

Knowledge check 7

Briefly outline and exemplify two reasons why the national turnout figure may not be a reliable indicator of the level of participation.

The rise in 'unconventional' participation

It is sometimes said that the UK is suffering from a **participation crisis**. The argument points to the decline in the number of people who are participating in politics as measured by conventional statistics. However, there are a number of factors to suggest that, rather than participation *declining*, it has changed direction and structure.

- Pressure group membership has grown. Friends of the Earth currently has an active global membership of over 2 million people in 76 countries; the Royal Society for the Protection of Birds has a UK membership of over 1.2 million — more than the membership of the three main parties combined.
- Demonstrations and public protests have risen in number as direct action tactics — most recently against tuition fees and austerity measures — provide opportunities for popular political expression.
- E-democracy is on the rise. A feature of modern political participation is the prevalence of social networking, innovative political communication (blogging and tweeting) and the rise of e-petitions — such as the request to bring forward the inquest of a victim of the Hillsborough disaster which reached the 100,000 signatures needed to force a parliamentary debate in November 2012.
- Many surveys indicate that due to the rise of information and communication technology, people are better informed about issues than at any previous point and are more likely to engage in activities from the 'conventional' such as donating money to causes they support, to the 'unconventional' such as buying or boycotting products for ethical reasons.

Participation crisis A common belief that political participation in the UK has declined to the extent that it threatens the state of democracy.

Knowledge check 8

Identify two recent examples of e-petitions that have led to parliamentary debates.

Summary

After studying this topic you should be able to:

- Understand and use basic political terms with confidence such as those relating to democracy, participation, legitimacy and representation.
- Be able to analyse with confidence the development of universal suffrage in the UK, including key milestones in the extension of the right to vote.
- Understand and evaluate issues regarding enfranchisement and the participation of key demographic groups — especially issues relating to gender, class, ethnicity and age.
- Explain and exemplify the different types of democracy — especially direct and representative democracy — and evaluate the UK's representative democracy.
- Evaluate and analyse the changing nature of political participation in the UK and the extent to which there is a 'participation crisis'.

◼ Elections and referendums

Representation and elections

What are the main functions of elections?

Elections are a fundamental part of the democratic process. They provide a means for eligible citizens to express political preferences, pass judgements on a party or government in office and vote for candidates to represent them in the decision-making process. The main functions of elections can be summarised as:

- Participation — elections provide the single most important opportunity for individuals to engage in the democratic process and influence the political agenda.
- Legitimisation — successful candidates and parties can claim an electoral mandate to pursue their policies and enact their manifesto commitments. Mandates can be personal (for an individual MP within a constituency) or for a party (winning enough seats to secure control of the Parliament).
- **Accountability** — elections offer citizens the chance to hold individual MPs to account and to pass a verdict on the performance of the government.
- Representation — in elections, citizens vote for people to act on their behalf in the decision-making process.

The nature of representation in the UK is contested. Some stress that representatives should be seen as trustees — rather than delegates, faithfully serving the wishes of their electors — who act on behalf of their constituents with a responsibility to use their experience and expertise when making judgements. Edmund Burke (1729–97), who was discussed in the previous section, supported this model, emphasising the importance of representatives using their own conscience and judgement. However, the advent of party loyalty, whipped votes and the extension of collective responsibility has severely diminished the Burkean trustee model in recent decades.

What is an electoral mandate?

An electoral mandate implies that the winning political party at a general election has obtained popular authority from the **electorate** and therefore the 'right' to govern in accordance with its electoral commitments, particularly through the passage of legislation and action detailed in its **manifesto**. An electoral mandate can be regarded as a contractual relationship between the winning party and the electorate as it contains elements of obligation on the part of the governing party.

However, the strength of the electoral mandate claimed by the UK's government is questionable since a winning party has never achieved over 50% of the popular vote in any postwar election. At times, the difference between the verdict of voters — in the form of the national vote — and how this translates into seats is quite stark:

- In 2005, Labour polled 35.2% of votes cast — the lowest share of the vote ever recorded by a party that was able to form a single party majority government, in this case with a very healthy working majority of 66 MPs.

Elections A mechanism of social and political choice that allows people to choose representatives to hold office and carry out particular functions.

Accountability Elections provide citizens with the chance to hold individual MPs and the government of the day accountable for their actions and conduct.

Knowledge check 9

Provide an example of how voters within a constituency have held an MP 'to account'.

Electorate Individuals entitled to vote because they qualify and are on the electoral register.

Manifesto A pre-election document drawn up by a political party and containing policies and legislation that will be carried out or enacted if the party is elected to government.

- In 2015, the Conservative Party's share of the vote rose just 0.8% from 2010 (rising from 36.1% to 36.9%) and yet it was able to exchange coalition government for single-party government with a working majority of 12 MPs.
- In 2017, the Labour Party received 12.8 million votes. In securing 40% of the popular vote, it gained a third more votes than it had received at the previous election. However, it won just 30 more seats, moving from 232 to 262.

The characteristics of different electoral systems used in the UK

What types of electoral systems are used in the UK?

There are several different ways of translating votes into seats at elections. Some systems used in the UK emphasise the formation of strong, single-party governments, while others stress the importance of an accurate translation of votes to seats.

The electoral systems used in the UK fit broadly into three types:

- **Majoritarian systems** require constituency winners to secure either the most votes (e.g. first past the post which is known as a '**plurality system**' since only a plurality — the largest amount — of votes is required) or an absolute majority (e.g. AV or SV). Twenty years ago virtually all UK-based elections, whether for the Westminster Parliament, local government or UK elections to the European Parliament, were majoritarian. First past the post (FPTP) is still used for elections to the Westminster Parliament. Another majoritarian system — SV — is used to elect the London mayor.
- Systems that are based on **proportional representation** look to secure as close a relationship as possible between votes won and seats gained. Some proportional systems (e.g. list systems) use large regional constituencies with multiple representatives to guarantee this. In Northern Ireland elections to local government, the Northern Ireland Assembly and the European Parliament take place under single transferable vote (STV) — a highly proportional electoral system — as have Scottish local elections since 2007. Since 1999, UK elections to the European Parliament have taken place under a closed regional party list system.
- **Hybrid systems** combine aspects of majoritarian and proportional systems. Some hybrid systems (e.g. additional member system) allow voters two votes — one for a constituency representative who requires a simple majority, and another for regional representation from a party list. Scottish Parliament and Welsh Assembly elections take place under a hybrid additional member system (AMS) known as first-past-the-post top-up. The Greater London Assembly's 25 members are also elected under an AMS system.

Plurality system An electoral system that requires a winning candidate to receive the most votes (rather than a majority) to win a seat.

Proportional representation Describes electoral systems that seek to apportion votes to seats in a proportional manner.

The performance of the UK's electoral systems

First past the post (FPTP)

How does FPTP work?

Under FPTP, voters are given a single vote which is not transferable. Votes within each constituency are then counted and the candidate who secures the largest number of votes wins. A candidate need only secure one vote more than their nearest rival (i.e. a simple majority or 'simple plurality') even where this will often be less than 50% of the total number of votes cast for all candidates.

In the UK, FPTP normally operates on the basis of single-member constituencies — that is where one individual is elected to represent one geographical area. In the June 2017 general election there were 650 such single-member constituencies. Where a vacancy occurs, as a result of the death or resignation of the incumbent, a **by-election** is held in the affected constituency/ward under the same FPTP electoral system.

What are the main advantages of FPTP?

For many people, MPs included, the FPTP electoral system is the most appropriate for the UK's democracy. Despite some apparent drawbacks, there are clearly valid reasons why the system has remained in use for such a long time. The central strengths of FPTP include:

- Representation — despite the adverse votes-to-seats ratio, the FPTP system is representative in a *geographical* sense. Each **constituency** within the UK is roughly the same size (containing approximately 70,000 voters) and has a single representative. Every winning candidate pledges to represent all constituents, rather than just those who voted for them, to the best of their ability.

- Equality of suffrage — another key strength is the fact that voters themselves have just one vote: they do not cast votes for a party and do not rank candidates according to preference. They only vote for single constituency candidates who may, or may not, represent one of the main parties.

- Accountability — twinned with fair and equal representation goes 'accountability'. The single-member nature of the system allows constituents to make clear statements in support or opposition of their constituency MPs and 'hold to account' those deemed unacceptable. (This pans out at a national level when governments are 'held to account' and voted out of office, such as the Conservatives in 1997, Labour in 2010 and the Lib Dems in 2015.) A 6% swing away from Labour from 2005 to 2010 saw it lose its majority along with nearly 100 seats. The Lib Dem vote share declined from 7.9% to 7.4% between 2015 and 2017 and yet its number of seats rose from 8 to 12.

- Decisive results and stable governments — the key strength, for supporters of the system, is the fact that it delivers decisive, single-party majority governments. With just two exceptions (those of 1974 and 2010) every postwar election has resulted in a single-party government — this is also true of 2017 with the caveat that a minority government was formed. As a result, the winning party is able to begin to fulfil its manifesto commitments and is able to be held singularly accountable for its successes or failures at the following general election.

- Marginalising 'extremists' — the system also sidelines extremist parties which is seen by many as a strength. The Liberal Democrats may well suffer (look no further than 2005 when over 20% of the vote share resulted in under 10% of the seats) but so too do parties with, arguably, a more disruptive or malign message. Some would point to UKIP's polling of over 3.8 million votes in the 2015 election, winning just one seat. Without the legitimacy of a strong parliamentary platform to demonstrate its post-referendum relevance, UKIP all but melted away in the 2017 general election.

By-election The election of a single constituency MP when a seat becomes vacant between general elections.

Exam tip

FPTP is most often referred to as a 'simple plurality system' rather than a 'majoritarian system'. Winning candidates do not need to achieve a majority of the votes (i.e. more than 50%), just the most votes within the constituency.

Constituency A geographical area that returns a representative to an assembly following an election.

Knowledge check 10

Provide an example from a pre-1997 election and a post-1997 election to illustrate FPTP delivering a 'decisive' result.

What are the main disadvantages of FPTP?

The key arguments for changing the system revolve around the fact that FPTP is both unrepresentative and unfair. Among other drawbacks, the system does not translate votes to seats accurately — it distorts voting values, it creates 'safe seats' and therefore votes of unequal value, and it perpetuates the unrepresentative nature of MPs. Some of the most potent disadvantages of FPTP include:

- It is unrepresentative — the FPTP system does not do what elections are fundamentally required to do: translate voters' wishes into a representative assembly in a democratic way. The most significant reason for this is the large number of **wasted votes**. Under a winner-takes-all system the size of a candidate's majority is ignored, as are all votes for losing candidates. Wasted votes can lead to serious electoral anomalies — in 1951 Labour polled 48.8% of the vote and won 295 seats while the Conservatives polled 48.0% of the vote and won 321 seats.

- It creates 'safe' seats and therefore uncompetitive elections with a disinclination for voters to turnout. In safe seats, odds are firmly stacked against any voters looking for change. Even sizeable swings — of up to 10% — from one candidate or party to another will not affect the outcome in an estimated 65% of constituencies in any given general election. When seats are known to be safe, the very 'British' phenomenon of tactical voting comes into play. Tactical voting is when a voter casts a vote not for their preferred candidate but for a less preferred candidate who has a better chance of winning. The usual reason is to keep out the candidate of a party that the voter particularly dislikes. The very existence of tactical voting in an electoral system — that voters feel they are casting a more effective vote for an alternative candidate to their favoured one — reflects deeply undemocratic flaws.

- Lack of representation among MPs themselves —FPTP requires that candidates are selected by local constituency associations, usually from head office 'approved' lists. Consequently, the white, middle-class male 'standard' has repeated itself to the detriment of a more balanced House. The 2017 House of Commons is being trumpeted as the most diverse ever — yet while the number of female and ethnic minority MPs are at their highest level (with 207 and 51 respectively), just 1% of the House of Commons are physically disabled, compared to 16% of the adult working-age population.

- Single-member constituencies — the major disadvantage with single-member constituencies is that supporters of other parties may not feel that they have a sympathetic representative to turn to.

- Unrewarding of 'minor' parties — traditionally (though not necessarily in 2015), Liberal Democrat support is fairly evenly spread across the country. The Conservatives and Labour on the other hand enjoy strong support in specific areas. The Liberal Democrats generally come second in well over a third of constituencies (around 250) but any votes for second place are, of course, wasted.

Wasted votes Votes cast for a candidate that did not win, or over what the winning candidate required to win a simple majority are regarded as 'wasted'.

Knowledge check 11

Research an example of a safe seat and explain why the phenomenon of safe seats can discourage turnout.

Alternative electoral systems: debates, issues, advantages and disadvantages

In order to properly evaluate the FPTP electoral system a good knowledge of the alternative systems used in the UK at non-Westminster elections is essential.

The supplementary vote (SV)

All **directly elected English mayors**, notably the mayor of London, and all police and crime commissioners are elected using the supplementary vote (SV) electoral system. SV is a majoritarian electoral system that allows voters to rank candidates in order of preference. Each voter has two votes, a first and second choice. If no candidate wins over 50% of the first-choice vote, all but the top two candidates are eliminated with the second choices on their ballot papers added to the first-choice votes already won by the two leaders. The final totals for the two leading candidates now must produce an outright winner.

> **Directly elected mayors** These are local government executives directly elected by the people within a local authority area.

Example

The system was used to elect the London mayor and in May 2016 winning candidate Sadiq Khan's 56.8% of the vote was based on first and second preferences as his vote share of 44.2% of first choices was not enough to win on the first round vote alone.

Advantages

- It is easy to understand.
- Voters have more choice than under FPTP and there are slightly fewer 'wasted' votes than under FPTP.
- It avoids third-placed candidates emerging victorious with lots of second preference ballots.

Disadvantages

- It is not proportional due to the presence of significant numbers of wasted votes.
- There is no need for an absolute majority — candidates may win without over 50% of first or second preferences.
- It encourages tactical voting with voters considering how best to deploy their votes in the event that their first choice gets eliminated.

Single transferable vote (STV)

The single transferable vote (STV) is a fully proportional voting system. It is complex, but favoured by many for its fairness and the amount of choice that it gives to voters. It dates from the 1850s, so it has stood the test of time. It is used in local and assembly elections in Northern Ireland. It is also the system operating in the Republic of Ireland and has been used for local government in Scotland from 2007.

STV works in the following way:

- Constituencies return more than one member each. In Northern Ireland, for example, the normal number is six.
- In order to be elected, a candidate must achieve a 'quota'. The quota is calculated by taking the total votes cast and dividing it by the number of seats plus one (i.e. if there are six seats, the number is seven; the whole result, plus one, is the quota).

$$Q = \left(\frac{\text{Total votes cast}}{\text{Number of seats} + 1} \right) + 1$$

- Voters may vote for all the candidates in their own order of preference. They do not *have* to vote for all candidates, but only the number they wish to select.

- Voters may vote for candidates from different parties and may show a preference between candidates of the same party.
- Candidates who achieve the quota on their first preference are elected. When that happens, their second and subsequent preferences are redistributed among the other candidates.
- When more candidates achieve the quota by adding redistributed votes to their first preferences, their spare votes are also redistributed. This continues until no more candidates can achieve the quota. At this point, the votes of the candidates at the bottom of the poll begin to have their subsequent preferences redistributed.
- When the required number of candidates has achieved the quota, the counting can end.

STV was selected for elections to the Northern Ireland Assembly for two reasons. First, it is used in the Republic of Ireland so was familiar and trusted and, second, it fitted the circumstances of a very divided community — one that had seen the FPTP voting system deny effective representation to many communities for many years.

Example

The most recent elections to the Northern Ireland Assembly under STV took place in March 2017 — the sixth round of elections since the Assembly was created. An example of this system's broad proportionality is seen in Sinn Fein — the second highest supported party — coming second and winning 27 of the 90 seats based on 28% of the national vote.

Advantages

- **Multi-member constituencies** mean that constituents have a better choice when seeking assistance and representatives are likely to be much more reflective of the voting population.
- A broadly proportional result is assured with fewer votes wasted.
- Greater voter choice and 'power to the people'.
- Likelihood of coalition government to unite divided communities.

Disadvantages

- The single MP-constituency link is removed.
- It is complicated for voters and involves a lengthy process of vote counting.
- Parties still retain much power in choosing which candidates stand in which seats.
- It can lead to weak coalitions and issues with accountability when considering how to pass electoral judgements on the performance of individual representatives.

Closed regional party list

The UK currently operates a closed regional list system to elect Members of the European Parliament. Under the list system, voters are offered a choice of political parties and the chance to vote for one of the party lists. The seats are awarded in proportion to the votes cast for each party. This is the most proportional of all systems and this is its greatest attraction.

List systems normally include a threshold or minimum proportion of the total votes which a party must receive to win any seats at all. In Germany, for example, where the similar AMS system was adopted after the Second World War, a high minimum threshold of 5% was adopted to prevent extremists gaining representation.

Multi-member constituencies A geographical area in which there is more than one representative, with representation usually based on the proportionality of the vote.

Knowledge check 12

Suggest two reasons why multi-member constituencies might offer better representation than single-member constituencies.

Using a *closed* list system, voters have no influence over which individuals are elected from the list and the order of the list is determined by the party leaderships. An *open* list on the other hand permits voters to see candidates within the list and indicate a preference for a certain candidate.

Example

In the European Parliamentary elections in May 2014, UKIP was the best supported party winning 24 out of 73 seats based on 26.6% of the vote.

Advantages

- The result is proportionate (as near as possible) often allowing smaller parties to benefit.
- By-elections do not occur — if a seat becomes vacant, a party simply fills the vacancy with whoever is on its list.
- Coalitions are often formed meaning the politics is more consensual.

Disadvantages

- Regional representation breaks the close links between constituents and their representatives, creating a 'democratic deficit' as voters do not choose or hold accountable any candidates.
- Parties have lots of power in determining the make-up of the lists.
- It can produce weak coalition governments.

The additional member system (AMS)

The additional member system (AMS) is used to elect regional representatives to the devolved bodies of the Scottish Parliament and the Welsh Assembly. AMS is known as a hybrid or mixed system, combining FPTP and a regional list system. Under AMS every voter has two votes: one is for a constituency candidate and one from a choice of party lists. AMS is something of a compromise, designed to preserve the strengths of parliamentary constituencies with individual MPs, but also to attempt to factor in party support to produce a much more proportional result than FPTP.

Under AMS in both Scotland and Wales, two-thirds of the seats are elected using FPTP with the other third elected on the basis of closed regional list voting. There is a significant extra element in the form of a complex calculation which adjusts the proportion of additional votes cast on the list system to give a more proportional result — parties which do less well in the constituencies (typically Conservatives or Greens) have their proportion of list votes adjusted upwards. Those who do proportionally well under FPTP (typically the Scottish National Party) have their list votes adjusted downwards.

In Scotland, the total number of MSPs is 129: 73 of these are voted in directly from constituencies under FPTP (exactly the same constituencies as used for Westminster general elections). However, 56 MSPs are 'additional' members and they come from eight Scottish regions (seven MSPs in each region).

In Wales, there are 60 members of the Assembly — 40 from constituencies and 20 'additional' members representing five regions.

> **Exam tip**
>
> Remember that proportional representation (PR) is not a voting system itself but a term to describe the proportional translation of votes to seats.

Example

In May 2016, the Scottish parliamentary elections saw the SNP win 64 of the 129 seats. It secured 59 of the 73 constituency seats based on a vote of 46.5%, but just 4 of the 56 regional additional member seats based on 41.7% of the vote.

Advantages

- Voters have two votes and therefore more choice and strong links between individual representatives and their constituencies still remain.
- AMS represents party support more accurately as the 'additional member' part redistributes seats to parties which perform less well in the FPTP vote. The most popular party also has a realistic chance of securing a majority of seats to form an effective single-party government.
- Minority and under-represented groups have better representation as parties can place them higher up the closed regional lists.

Disadvantages

- However, the system is clearly more complex than simple FPTP as it involves formulae to translate votes to seats.
- AMS often results in coalitions (e.g. Germany), but these tend to be stable and not made up of many different parties.
- Additional members do not have a specific constituency and therefore are not directly accountable to a set of electors — AMS creates two different types of representative.

> **Knowledge check 13**
>
> Explain why the Conservative Party wins most of its Scottish Parliamentary seats in the form of additional members.

Patterns of voting behaviour

The decline of long-term factors

Long-term factors that influence political engagement and electoral participation — gender, social class, ethnicity and age — were discussed in the section on 'Democracy and participation'.

In many ways, the easiest way to explain voting behaviour is to think about long-term (primacy) and short-term (recency) factors — where primacy factors may predispose an individual to support a particular political party and recency factors may moderate their outlook. To summarise:

- **The 'primacy' model** suggests that longer-term factors are more important than short-term factors in deciding elections. Supporters of this view tend to see stability in electoral behaviour as opposed to volatility.
- **The 'recency' model** holds that voting patterns are in fact more volatile and that processes such as embourgeoisement have led to class and partisan dealignment. As a result, short-term factors are much more important, with as many as 10 million voters making up their minds in the last month of the general election campaign.

Evidence of voting behaviour in many modern industrial nations points to a shift away from group/party voting of one kind or another. We have seen the decline in 'class voting' (through dealignment and/or embourgeoisiement) over recent decades alongside the weakening of traditional patterns and the growth in voter volatility. Voters, rather than blindly following patterns that have pre-existed for decades, are much more rational in the way they cast their votes. Voters may reflect more objectively on the parties and their policies, the leaders themselves, and as **floating voters** be far more amenable to messages within the electoral campaign itself.

The rise of short-term factors

Party policies

Voters who reflect more carefully on party policies are more likely to be **issue voting**. Issue voting separates into what David Denver writing in 2011 referred to as 'position' or 'valence' voting: 'Position issues are those on which people can take positions (for or against public ownership of industries, for example). Valence issues are issues on which nearly everyone takes the same side.' Such explanations stress the significance of short-term factors within recent models of voting behaviour, highlighting particularly the importance of party policies, party leaders, election campaigns and the influence of the media.

- In the 2015 general election, issues at stake were focused firmly on health, the economy and immigration. According to a YouGov poll in the month prior to the 2015 general election, 50% of the public said that 'health' was one of the most important issues affecting the public. However, for many voters there appeared little to choose between the two parties and the election result yielded little overall change.

- The 2017 general election campaign was hailed as a return to ideological politics with voters finding that genuine alternatives were presented to them — party policies varied significantly in terms of attitudes to EU immigrants, taxation rates, tuition fees, schools policies and health and social care. The election saw turnout rise to its highest level for 20 years.

Party leaders

It must be remembered that the UK system is very different from most modern democratic states in that the political head of state is not directly elected by the people. After such a relentless media focus on the qualities and characteristics of the leaders during the campaign, many voters find themselves confused on election day, faced with a ballot paper populated by constituency hopefuls, and no prime minister. However, as indirect as it might be, the relative popularity of party leaders can have serious consequences for the party's electoral prospects.

- Margaret Thatcher's authoritative leadership attracted significant numbers of voters to the Conservative Party in general elections between 1979 and 1987, especially in contrast to the unconventional Labour leader Michael Foot in 1983.

- The popularity of Tony Blair swept many other Labour MPs into Parliament in 1997 and 2001 leading to Labour's two landslide electoral victories.

- The personal unpopularity of Nick Clegg in 2015 saw his Liberal Democrats reduced to a parliamentary party of just 8 MPs.

- The perceived aloofness and reserve of Theresa May was exposed on the campaign trail in 2017 and floating voters — many of whom had backed UKIP, drawn to the 'straight-talking' leadership style of Nigel Farage, in the previous general election — did not uniformly back the Conservatives.

But the significance of 'leadership' can also be misleading and overstated. Prior to the 2017 general election, YouGov polls asked London voters who would make the

---

Floating voter An individual who does not identify strongly with one party or another, and is likely to be influenced by short-term issues and the campaign itself.

Exam tip

Use the correct vocabulary wherever possible — 'recency factors' and 'primacy factors' are effective political terms to use in this context.

Issue voting Voters who are more rational in the way they cast their vote are less likely to feel constrained by long-term factors and more likely to scrutinise the stance of the main parties over key issues that affect them.

Knowledge check 14

Explain with examples the term 'rational voting'.

'best prime minister' — of course a very different question from the one that voters would be faced with in a constituency-based general election just a few days later. In YouGov's leadership poll at this time, Jeremy Corbyn had a lead of 3% (37% to 34%) over Theresa May, but Theresa May won the popular vote by the same difference.

Party campaigns

It is difficult to establish firm evidence for the significance of **election campaigns** in determining patterns of voting behaviour. First, many voters have a clear intention to vote a certain way prior to the campaign even starting. Second, while some voters may 'firm up' their choices during the campaign, it is difficult to establish whether this can be attributed to the persuasiveness of the campaign itself. And third, if the final weeks leading up to a general election do indeed see more 'undecideds' fall into line behind a particular party, with the rise of unorthodox communication and social media platforms, it is almost impossible to know whether they were persuaded by the more formal elements of party-orchestrated election campaigns or not.

The impact of election campaigns also depends on context. Where the outcome is unclear, or when the election is called unexpectedly, the campaign can take on an even greater significance. In addition, campaigns can see less 'swing' and more '**churn**' — less discernible or evident movement in a single direction, and more volatility hidden within broadly stable headline figures.

Reliable estimates put the figure of 'undecideds', and therefore voters *more likely to be persuaded* by the campaign itself at 20% of total voters. The 2017 general election saw significant late and campaign-based fluctuations — the Labour deficit (of 20% according to some pre-campaign polls) was cut back to less than 3% at the ballot box. The energy of Jeremy Corbyn, the perceived coldness of Theresa May, the presentation of the parties' manifestos and the ability to energise groups of previously stay-at-home voters proved to be the difference.

Election campaigns
A general election campaign historically lasts 17 formal days — between Parliament being dissolved and polling day. In 2017 the campaign lasted 5 weeks.

Churn Movement in opinion polls during the campaign is known as 'churn'. Churning is not especially decisive unless many voters churn in one direction.

The influence of the media on electoral outcomes

The true influence of the media in influencing electoral outcomes is contested. Issues and debates tend to focus on three key areas:

- The extent to which the broadcast media, and especially the BBC, are biased, seeking to trivialise radical issues or outsiders that challenge the status quo.
- The extent to which traditional print journalism has been replaced by 'new' media channels of the internet and social media platforms — with the inherent risk of the wide consumption of unreliable (even 'fake') news.
- The extent to which opinion polls — themselves increasingly unreliable in an age of greater voter volatility — shape opinion rather than reflecting it.

Are the 'traditional' media biased?

A variety of theories of voting behaviour stress the impact of the traditional media in shaping the way that people vote and subsequent electoral outcomes. 'Dominant ideology' theories emphasise that since the traditional mass media — especially television news corporations and conventional print journalism — are controlled by a narrow metropolitan elite, the broad objective is to encourage readers or watchers to preserve the established status quo, trivialising 'radical' issues and portraying policies 'alternative' to the mainstream in a negative light.

Proponents of this view point to the treatment that Nigel Farage and UKIP have experienced in recent years. Supporters of UKIP's 'right of centre' views pointed to how the traditional media had dismissed or ridiculed the party and its leader, in ways that ultimately proved to be markedly out-of-touch with the party's support at large.

In keeping with this, the 'hegemonic theory' of media manipulation highlights the disproportionate number of media workers with liberal, middle-class upbringings and outlooks, that bring a pronounced bias to their work, however unintentional this might be. This theory stresses that the prevailing order (or hegemony) is preserved through a consistent and prolonged reinforcement of the power relationships and cultural norms within the state.

In recent years the BBC has come in for some significant criticism too. It is claimed that the BBC is left-leaning, pro-EU and anti-business. In the last few years, the BBC Trust has funded independent research into the corporation's output to verify the BBC's claim to impartiality. Most recently, research was undertaken by Cardiff University, looking at two distinct years — 2007 and 2012 and two specific claims:

- On accusations that the BBC is left-leaning, research instead found that while Labour and the Conservatives do dominate political coverage, accounting for 86% of appearances in 2007 and 80% in 2012, the Conservatives actually get more airtime than Labour. Gordon Brown as prime minister may have outnumbered David Cameron in appearances but only by a ratio of less than two to one (47 vs 26) in 2007. In contrast in 2012, David Cameron outnumbered Ed Milliband by a factor of nearly four to one (53 vs 15). In terms of impact on electoral outcomes, David Cameron's Conservative Party was 'successful' in both 2010 and 2015.

- On accusations that the BBC is pro-EU, the research looked at 2007 in which the Lisbon Treaty dominated the agenda absorbing 70% of EU coverage, and 2012 which focused on negotiations over ratifying the EU budget which accounted for 72% of EU coverage. In both cases the debate was dominated by the representatives of the two main parties and the EU was framed narrowly as a threat to British interests.

What has been the impact of the rise of 'new' media on electoral outcomes?

It is widely reported and perceived, though perhaps less widely understood, that 'new' internet-based media — and especially the social media platforms of Twitter, Facebook and also YouTube — have changed the way that participatory democracy functions, the way that elected officials interact with the public and, consequently, the outcome of elections. Social media enable individuals to 'connect' with millions of others instantaneously. Donald Trump — a prolific user of Twitter in his presidential election campaign in 2016 said: 'I like it because I can get my point of view out there, and my point of view is very important to a lot of people that are looking at me.'

Key ways that social media can influence electoral outcomes include:

- Social media facilitate direct contact between those seeking election and voters — bypassing orthodox media channels and conventional advertising. In the 2017 general election, Labour's younger and more tech-savvy supporters had pre-built extensive support bases for blogs and social media accounts to utilise during the campaign to communicate pro-Corbyn coverage, with memes and Facebookfriendly headlines (e.g. 'The systematic Tory abuse of disabled people') which reached tens of thousands of people.

- Social media allow key messages to go viral and reach even larger audiences — like-minded voters and activists can 'share' news, memes, information and campaign events. In the 2016 US presidential election the marginal news website Breitbart broke into the mainstream with posts that went viral, becoming a very prominent supporter of Donald Trump's right-wing campaign messages.
- Use of social media 'analytics' enables messages to be tailored to audiences so that different genders, regions or ages can receives slightly different messages.
- Social media 'controversies' can have disastrous consequences and numerous politicians have been undone by intemperate tweets. In 2014 Emily Thornberry resigned her shadow attorney general position after notoriously tweeting a photograph of a white van outside a house with three England flags alongside the caption 'image from Rochester'.
- The practical power of social media is significant too — it has enabled many more obscure politicians to raise significant campaign funds, and for 'ordinary' voters to leverage their substantial support to combat the dominance of traditional, moneyed interests.

A more malign side of internet-based media is that unregulated and unreliable 'fake news' has become a recent phenomenon. Internet giants Google and Facebook increasingly fund fact-checkers — through organisations such as Full Fact and First Draft — to protect the general election from false reports or misleading claims gaining traction on social media.

Do opinion polls reflect public opinion or shape electoral outcomes?

Opinion polls have become a central feature of electoral life. In 2017 the majority of the pre-election polling data were generated by five main organisations — YouGov, ICM, IPSOS/MORI, ComRes and Survation. Polling companies generally claim that 95% of the time, a poll of 1,000 people will be accurate within a margin of error of +/–3%. This means that a party's figure could be up to three percentage points higher or lower than that shown in the poll.

However, while opinion polls may well serve the vital function of informing politicians about the current views and priorities of selected groups of people, and allowing voters to see how others are engaging with parties and policies, they have been criticised for a number of reasons:

- The inaccuracy of polls prior to the 2015 and 2017 general elections — most notably polling predictions in the UK prior to the 2015 general election, the EU referendum and in the US presidential election in 2016 — has been a cause of concern. However, while this called into question the very purpose of polling data, it also confirmed to many that their impact on determining outcomes was negligible.
- The 2015 and 2017 general elections saw such a pronounced focus on the fluctuations of opinion polls that detailed discussion of party policies was said to have taken a 'back seat'. In the 6 weeks of the 2015 general election campaign a total of 92 voting intention polls were conducted and publicised — very few of which came anywhere near the actual outcome of a Conservative victory.

Opinions polls A sample-based survey of public opinion providing data on popular voting intentions, party leaders or party policies.

■ Many countries — including France, Canada, Norway and Greece — have some kind of ban on the dissemination of pre-election polling data. The concern in several of these countries is that if opinion polling data were permitted, undecided voters would simply join a 'bandwagon' and add their vote to the momentum of the polls.

The nature and use of referendums in the UK

For several generations in the postwar era, referendums were viewed as being incompatible with the UK's political culture. Clement Attlee, prime minister in the 1940s, seemed to articulate this most clearly, referring to referendums as 'a tool of demagogues and dictators' and 'alien to our traditions'. Since 1997 however, the UK has experienced UK-wide referendums on the voting system and membership of the EU, regional referendums on the powers of devolved bodies, and local referendums on congestion charges and local mayors — to name but a few examples (see Table 4).

Table 4 Examples of referendums

Level	Date	Location	Referendum	Result
Local	February 2005	Edinburgh	Traffic congestion charging	No 74:26
Local	May 2012	Birmingham (and several other cities)	To create a democratically elected mayor	No 58:42
Regional	March 2011	Wales	To extend the law-making powers of the Welsh Assembly	Yes 63:37
Regional	October 2015	Scotland	Whether Scotland should become independent	No 55:45
National	May 2011	UK	AV as a replacement electoral system for FPTP	No 68:32
National	June 2016	UK	Should the UK remain part of the EU	No 52:48

What are referendums and why are they used?

A referendum is a vote on a single issue put before the electorate by the government, usually in the form of a question requiring a yes or no response. There is much debate on their constitutional position as they are a feature of direct democracy at odds with the UK's system of representative democracy.

Referendums are used or held for a number of reasons:

■ **To legitimise and entrench major constitutional changes.** The UK's uncodified constitution and the principle of parliamentary sovereignty mean that Parliament has the power to make and unmake laws and change the relationship between the government and the governed at any time. A popular vote in support of an institution or policy however effectively entrenches the decision.

■ **To ensure public consultation.** Some referendums arise from a genuine desire on the part of government to engage or to enthuse the public for a scheme or significant change.

■ **To put proposals to the electorate.** Governments (or prospective governments, if the referendum is a manifesto commitment) can steer clear of committing to difficult policies which might alienate voters. The Labour government consistently promised a referendum prior to adopting the euro — thereby freeing the administration from making a decision either way — and the Conservative Party long pledged a referendum on the UK's relationship with the European Union before committing to it in 2016.

Synoptic link

Referendums around the world

In some areas of the world, for example Switzerland and California, referendums are frequent, sometimes styled as initiatives or propositions since many of them originate with the people.

- Switzerland has several referendums each year. Three took place on 12 February 2017 on whether to allow easier naturalisation of third-generation immigrants, whether to create a national fund for roads and urban infrastructure and whether to overhaul the tax code.
- In California initiatives often come in the form of ballot propositions. In order to be considered, they require the signatures of 8% (for the amendments of the state constitution) and 5% (for a statute) of the number of people who voted for the most recent election of the governor. In November 2016, 17 such initiatives were included on the presidential election ballot in California legalising Marijuana (Proposition 64 passed) and abolishing the death penalty (Proposition 62 failed).

Knowledge check 16

Explain how referendums can entrench a political decision.

What did we learn about referendums from the 'Brexit' vote?

The Commons Public Administration and Constitutional Affairs Committee (**PACAC**) published its report *Lessons Learned from the EU Referendum* in April 2017. In it, the Committee confirmed that referendums have become a permanent part of the UK's democratic system, and to that end the Committee sought to clarify their role and purpose.

PACAC The body that examines constitutional issues and the quality and standards of administration within the Civil Service.

The Committee highlighted a key difference in the 'use' of referendums — supporting their use for the resolution of key constitutional differences but opposing what the Committee termed 'bluff call' referendums, when they are used to close down an unwanted debate, using the example of David Cameron's calling of the EU referendum.

As far as the functioning of the EU referendum, the Committee noted that it was on an enormously complex scale. Even so, it was run well and the result was technically sound. A number of significant issues, however, were highlighted, pertinent to any evaluation of the future use of referendums:

- The registration deadline date of 7 June saw a collapse of the voter registration website when over 515,000 people attempted to register. The government referred to unprecedented demand, but 38% (over 200,000) were duplicate registrations — partly down to the fact that there was no mechanism for a voter to check whether they were already registered, and partly down to the possibility of a cyber-attack, with botnets created to make multiple applications and evidence of a malicious subversion of the process.

- The 'designation' process (the endorsement of 'official' groups that would receive state funds) suffered from a lack of clarity and the delay in making the announcement on designation caused uncertainty and led to problems for fundraising and the continuity of campaigning.

- The tone and veracity of the advice and information provided to the public — especially that of the Treasury's inaccurate predictions of the economic consequences; the £9.3 million cost of a leaflet to all households advocating a 'Remain' vote, which undermined public confidence in the civil service; and most especially the Leave campaign's notable claim that leaving the EU would divert £350 million to the National Health Service.

- The complete lack of contingency planning was in stark contrast to the intensive programme prepared by Whitehall in 1975 for the possibility of the UK's exit from the Common Market. Planning appeared to be limited to the Treasury's gloomy forecasts for the UK's financial stability in the event of a leave vote, and the government's official position was that there would be no contingency planning.

Should referendums be used more widely?

The formation of the coalition government in 2010 saw a renewed drive for future referendums, with pledges to hold them on Welsh devolution, electoral reform, the relationship between the UK and the European Union and directly elected mayors. It also included the possibility that future referendums — at least at a local level — could take the form of 'initiatives' on issues prompted by the public.

Yes, referendums should be used more widely:

- Referendums can 'bridge the gap' between elections. Major constitutional changes are effectively protected or 'entrenched' by referendum success.

- Referendums provide a specific mandate for action. Local referendums can allow citizens to engage with important issues that affect them directly.

No, referendums should not be used more widely:

- Referendums are fundamentally at odds with representative democracy, under which decision making is handed over to elected representatives with greater expertise. Referendums are often associated with low turnout — their growing prevalence merely increasing apathy. Referendums require the reduction of complex and intricate issues to a simple yes or no question.

- They are expensive — the AV referendum in May 2011 is estimated to have cost over £75 million.

- In keeping with Clement Attlee's claim (that referendums are 'the devices of demagogues and dictators'), governments decide whether to hold referendums and how the question will be framed to ensure the best possible outcome for them.

Summary

After studying this topic you should be able to:
- Analyse the roles that elections play within a democracy.
- Understand, explain and evaluate the workings of the different electoral systems that operate in the UK — their strengths and weaknesses within certain contexts such as party support, voter choice and effective representation.
- Evaluate patterns of voting behaviour, especially long- and short-term factors.
- Understand the context of 'issue' or 'rational' voting and the parts played by such things as policies, leaders and election campaigns.
- Distinguish between direct and representative democracy and demonstrate a strong knowledge of the use of referendums in the UK, being able to evaluate arguments for their wider use.

Political parties

The origins, ideas, development and current policies of the main parties

The origins of political parties in the UK

We can understand political parties as groups of people with shared ideas, principles and values. Parties are usually also characterised as having:

- formal organisational structures — a leadership (with clearly set out mechanisms for electing or selecting leaders) and a membership
- formal processes for the development of policy and the selection and promotion of candidates
- objectives to turn their ideas and policies into government

So central are parties to the political process that they are only absent in territories within which dictatorial regimes suppress any form of coherent opposition. However, that is not to say that parties have always been with us. In the UK, prior to the 1832 Great Reform Act and the extension of the franchise, political activity within Parliament was dominated by 'factions' — loose groupings of like-minded individuals bound together by friendship, money and family ties. These factions lacked the characteristics of modern parties (such as internal party discipline or mass memberships). MPs at this time broadly identified themselves as Whigs or Tories.

With the widening of the franchise, the need to organise and to engage the expanding electorate became apparent. Over the course of the nineteenth century, Whigs and Tories developed into the more formally known Liberal Party and Conservative Party. As the franchise extended further around the beginning of the twentieth century, incorporating working men for the first time, the Labour Party was formed, not from a parliamentary faction but from the trade union movement which sought working-class representation within the House of Commons.

Knowledge check 17

Explain how the extension of the franchise changed political parties in the UK.

The Conservative Party

Party origins

The loosely organised Tory Party that existed prior to the 1830s evolved quite quickly into the modern Conservative Party following the 1832 Reform Act. Robert Peel's subsequent 'Tamworth Manifesto' in 1834 was credited as laying down the party's core principles. Often referred to as the 'party of government' the Conservative Party has dominated the political landscape in the UK. It was in office for 67 years of the twentieth century. In the nearly 40 years since 1979, it has been out of office for just 13 years, between 1997 and 2010.

One-nation conservatism

The ideological origins of the Conservative Party lie in 'conservatism' — gradual, pragmatic, evolutionary change while preserving existing institutions and political traditions. The adoption of a paternalistic approach in the twentieth century stressed centralised authority alongside 'compassionate' policies to support the disadvantaged. In the postwar period, one-nation conservatism embraced a mixed economy that combined free competition with state intervention, a universal welfare state and increasing European integration.

Thatcherism

In the 1970s and 1980s the Conservative Party adopted a 'New Right' stance by blending aspects of traditional conservatism (family values, national sovereignty) with a liberal approach to economics — privatisation, union controls, curbing the role of the state, sometimes referred to as **neo-liberalism**. This lurch to the right, a deviation from previous conservative positions dubbed **neo-conservatism**, caused fractures in the Conservative Party — Thatcher termed her supporters 'dry', and one-nation Tory opponents 'wet' — in a way that the party has found difficult to resolve.

The main ideas of the New Right can be summarised as:

- commitment to a free market economy — restricted state intervention, government interference and trade union power
- privatisation of publicly-owned industries such as gas, electricity, water and telecommunications
- reduction in direct taxation — income and corporation tax levels were reduced in a bid to incentivise work, business and entrepreneurship
- a 'neo-conservative' approach to law and order, emphasising moral authority and traditional institutions such as marriage
- limits on welfare support (targeting a supposed 'dependency culture') and an emphasis on self-reliance, home ownership and enterprise.

'New' conservatism under Cameron

The twenty-first century brought new economic challenges that reshaped the Conservative Party. In the years running up to the 2010 election, a healthy poll lead over Labour reduced the need to modernise and allowed a departure from previous policies to 'detoxify' the Tory image. Traditional focuses on law and order and immigration were blended with right-wing policies to cut spending and reduce the

Neo-liberalism An ideology that stresses the importance of the free market, individual rights and limited government.

Neo-conservatism Largely based on 1980s US commitments to maintaining traditional, Christian positions on law, order and morality and a resistance to freedoms that could lead to disorder and moral decay.

deficit. David Cameron's 'civic conservatism' lay in the 'Big Society' agenda which was criticised for replacing state support with uncertain levels of voluntarism.

The Conservative Party from 2015

The events of 2015–16 will live long in the political consciousness for many reasons, and the Conservative Party certainly experienced its fair share of turbulence and upheaval. Promising a referendum on continued EU membership, Cameron resigned following the 'No' vote. The subsequent leadership election initially pitted former allies Michael Gove and Boris Johnson against one another. Theresa May eventually emerged unchallenged and while withdrawal from the EU casts a long shadow over possible commitments, a number of early policy directions are:

- a commitment to deficit reduction and a balanced budget by the middle of the next decade, according to their 2017 manifesto
- curbs on local and regional government, limiting the proliferation of directly elected mayors
- reshaping government departments towards international trade and concentrating control of central government through cabinet committees

However, Theresa May's gamble in holding a general election in June 2017 backfired and the Tories lost their parliamentary majority necessitating a major rethink on many aspects of their pre-election manifesto.

The Labour Party

Party origins

The Labour Party was founded at the start of the twentieth century as the Labour Representation Committee. While a number of societies and federations aligned themselves, the trade union movement — primarily the Trades Union Congress (TUC) — provided the basis for its foundation, and substantially funds the Labour Party to this day.

Social democracy

The Labour Party's initial objective was to provide effective representation for the working classes and while never a purely 'socialist' party, the party's roots are most closely associated with socialism — an ideological tradition that stresses equality and cooperation. Labour's brand of social democracy emphasises the reform of capitalism, rather than its replacement. Policies focus on wealth redistribution and the modification of 'unfettered capitalism' through progressive economic policies that enhance equality.

It was the decision to grant all men over the age of 21 the vote in 1918 that transformed the Labour Party into a serious electoral force. The adoption of the party's 1918 constitution — stressing public ownership of key industries (within Clause IV) and emphasising the redistribution of wealth — provided the basis for future electoral success. In the 1922 general election, the party won 142 seats. A year later in 1923 the party took office for the first time as Ramsey Macdonald led a Labour-Liberal coalition government.

The postwar Labour Party

UK politics in the decades following 1945 was profoundly shaped by the creation of the welfare state and by policies that reached consensus over the need for a

Knowledge check 18

Explain with examples two ways that David Cameron changed the policies and approach of the Conservative Party from 2005.

Exam tip

Ensure that you can analyse and explain the main current policies of the Conservative Party with effective contemporary examples.

mixed economy to balance public and private ownership. A managed economy and a commitment to social justice through universal welfare, funded by progressive taxation, became the hallmarks of the Labour Party until the 1980s.

New Labour

Labour's lurch to the left — culminating in its 1983 election manifesto dubbed 'the longest suicide note in history' — and four electoral defeats to the Conservative Party between 1979 and 1992 led to a rebranding process and the birth of 'New Labour' under Tony Blair. New Labour saw the party distancing itself from the class conflict, 'left-wing', collectivist approaches of the traditional 'Old' Labour Party. Instead it stressed a '**Third Way**' through:

- An emphasis on the role of the individual rather than a focus on equality through collective action and shared ownership.
- An acceptance of the free market. The removal of Clause IV, along with its commitment to renationalisation, broadened the party's appeal but led to accusations that fundamental socialist principles had been abandoned.
- Adapting the welfare state to focus on education and health, and a targeted approach to welfare benefits, withholding them from those not actively seeking work.

The Labour Party in opposition, 2010–

Ed Miliband's leadership from 2010 sought to reposition the party as a credible alternative to the budget-cutting coalition government. But Miliband's initial heavy reliance on trade union support impeded wider appeal. The crushing electoral defeat of 2015 left the party in confusion. Those committed to a New Labour model blamed Miliband's retreat from it; others viewed the process of modernisation itself as a 'sell-out' for traditional Labour voters.

Jeremy Corbyn's leadership credentials were entirely different from those preceding him. Corbyn had spent many decades following a left-wing socialist agenda that had often put him at odds with the Labour leadership. With a lengthy record of backbench rebellion, Corbyn's late but overwhelmingly successful leadership challenge appeared to many stunned critics to be focused far more on opposition to modernisers within the Labour Party than on opposition to the Conservative Party in office. Consequently, his efforts to present a coherent, disciplined resistance to the government proved challenging.

- Supporters of Jeremy Corbyn's leadership emphasise his commitment to fair welfare, NHS spending, an environmental agenda and a positive programme of public service investment.
- Opponents highlight ineffectual and backward-looking leadership of a divided party that appears out of touch with the complex aspirations and concerns of the modern electorate.
- Opponents and supporters point to the 2017 election campaign to prove their respective points. While supporters point to the late surge in Labour support, the energy of the campaign and the party's renewed focus on fair taxation and state intervention, opponents question how, after 7 years of 'cuts and austerity', an incumbent party could raise its vote share by nearly 5% and an opposition party only secure 262 seats.

Third Way An emphasis on the ideological position that sits between traditional socialism and free capitalism — a blend of 'middle-class' concerns for rising living standards and social mobility alongside a well-functioning welfare state.

Knowledge check 19

What is social democracy?

The Liberal Democrats

The Liberal Democrats, 1988–2010

The modern Liberal Democrats have their recent roots in the formal merger of the Social Democratic Party and the Liberal Party that took place under the **Gang of Four** in 1988. Their principles stress the importance of the individual within the classical liberal traditions of the nineteenth century, alongside a modern focus on the effective provision of state-run educational and health systems, on individual rights, electoral reforms and reforms to the process of government.

Significant electoral success was established and consolidated in the 1990s and early 2000s, under leaders Paddy Ashdown and the late Charles Kennedy. In 2005, the party won 18.3% of the vote, rising to 23% under Nick Clegg's leadership in the 2010 general election.

Coalition government, 2010–15

The 5-year period between the general elections held in 2010 and 2015 marked an astonishing reversal of fortune for the Liberal Democrats. Despite winning less than 9% of the MPs in the House of Commons in 2010, the party's impressive share of the national vote, together with the Conservative Party's failure to secure an outright Commons majority, saw the Liberal Democrats under Nick Clegg becoming junior coalition partners with the Conservatives. The party's agenda was one of enhanced civil liberties and constitutional reforms, as well as attempting to style itself as an effective brake on the more austerity-minded Conservative Party.

Post-2015

The Liberal Democrats experienced as close to a total wipeout in 2015 as modern British electoral politics has conspired to provide. Opinion polls had indicated their likely demise, but the party's collapse from stable coalition partner to having just 8 MPs (receiving 4 million fewer votes than in the previous election) was momentous indeed. Under Tim Farron's leadership (elected in July 2015 following Clegg's resignation) the party's Commons presence grew by one after its victory in the Richmond Park by-election and climbed to 12 from 2017 — an election followed almost immediately by the resignation of Farron as leader. Sir Vince Cable, party leader from 20 June 2017 and the oldest leader of a political party since Winston Churchill, resolved to push for innovative solutions to public sector reforms, housing, taxation and business enterprise, believing that his party should occupy the 'vast middle ground' between the UK's two main parties.

Party structures and functions

Political parties lie at the heart of politics, dominating policy making, government decision making and ideological debate. They provide a platform for aspiring politicians and national leaders and are constantly evolving and adapting to balance the representative and governing roles expected of them. Yet political parties in the UK are often criticised for failing to fulfil their most basic functions:

- Falling electoral turnout is blamed on parties being insufficiently appealing to voters.
- Declining party membership is seen as evidence of their inability to engage with and enthuse ordinary people in policy formulation.

Gang of Four With the Labour Party in disarray four prominent MPs — Bill Rodgers, Roy Jenkins, Shirley Williams and David Owen — left it to form the Social Democratic Party.

Exam tip

Better examination responses will identify tensions and factions *within* the main UK parties and not simply between them.

Political party A group or association of people holding similar political views with an objective to implement their views through government.

■ Politicians are increasingly seen as 'slaves' to their parties, unable to vote with their consciences and tightly bound by collective responsibility.

This perceived failure is occurring against a confusing backdrop: a narrowing media focus on party leaders alongside the advancement of minor and nationalist parties to erode the traditional two-party system.

The functions of political parties

Despite criticisms, political parties perform several important functions:

■ **Representation** — of different views and opinions in society. This was particularly true in the era of high partisan alignment, but dealignment and the broadening appeal of modern **'catch-all' parties** has undermined this.

■ **Participation** — encouraging involvement in elections at various levels. Parties perform valuable educative functions — informing citizens of the issues that affect them and offering potential solutions.

■ **Policy making** — parties turn ideas into potential policy and legislation. The process of formulating, discussing, agreeing and presenting coherent policy options to the electorate is vital within a pluralist democracy.

■ **Government** — party organisation sustains government and opposition. The stability and coherence that parties provide allows for the operation of government and the parliamentary system.

■ **Political recruitment** — parties recruit and promote political leaders. Rigorous candidate selection processes weed out unsuitable candidates, but the major parties are increasingly criticised for drawing on ever-smaller pools of 'talent' dominated by career politicians.

Structures and functions (1): local and national organisation

The Conservative Party

The two main parties have similar local structures. For the Conservative Party, constituency associations play the largest role in organising members, mobilising support, planning election campaigns and selecting parliamentary candidates (following central office guidelines). Below constituency level, party branches are aligned to council wards to conduct similar activities on a smaller — and more local — level.

Nationally, the Conservative Campaign Headquarters (CCHQ) is based at Millbank, Westminster.

The Labour Party

Similar to the Conservative Party, most activities are coordinated on a constituency level. Individual members are assigned to a local branch — the lowest level of the party organisation and where candidates are selected for local elections. Delegates from local branches attend meetings of the General Committee of the Constituency Labour Party (CLP), the body that takes the lead in local and national election campaigns and plays a part in selecting candidates for parliamentary elections. In recent years, the importance of constituency party leaders has declined as reforms to internal party decision making, in favour of a one-member-one-vote (**OMOV**) system, have enhanced the clout of regular members.

'Catch-all' parties
Major parties in the UK are criticised for moving to the centre ground, bidding to appeal to as many voters as possible.

Knowledge check 20
Briefly explain the main functions of political parties in the UK.

Exam tip
Link specific functions of political parties with wider concepts, incorporating examples of how parties enhance democracy, representation and participation.

OMOV Relating to post-1993 Labour Party reforms and especially the replacement of the trade union 'block' vote for one member one vote in party business.

On a national level, the **National Executive Committee (NEC)** enforces party discipline, has the final say on the selection of parliamentary candidates, and oversees the preparation of policy proposals. Up to the 1990s, the annual conference was the party's sovereign policy-making body. In recent decades, decisions made at the party conference have been largely advisory.

Structures and functions (2): policy formulation

The Conservative Party

The long-established tradition within the Conservative Party sees the leader, along with a handful of key advisors, determining policy and formulating the party's election manifesto. This was certainly true up to the turn of the twenty-first century, with John Major notably maintaining as recently as 1992 that the party's manifesto 'was all me'. This top-down approach is tempered by the expectation that significant factions and groups — such as the **1922 Committee** and frontbench members — are able to contribute, but recent Conservative manifestos are widely agreed to have been drawn up by the party leaders themselves along with a handful of trusted advisors.

The Labour Party

While Labour Party conferences of the past saw genuinely collective policy making, reforms of the mid-1990s replaced the annual conference with a 2-year policy-making cycle, and shifted the responsibility of the conference to that of 'approving' policy already made and formalised by the National Executive Committee. In fact, the process has further centralised recently (and become far more akin to the Conservative Party) with Ed Milliband and a narrow team of senior MPs and academics widely credited with the writing of the 2010 and 2015 manifestos.

In 2017, despite *Daily Telegraph* claims that 100 policies demanded by the trade unions were included in the party's general election manifesto, the party retained its traditional meeting (dubbed a Clause V meeting after the 1918 constitution which requires it), during which pre-drafted policies — drawn up by party leaders and close advisors — were agreed.

The Liberal Democrats

In terms of prospects for grassroots members to be involved in the policy-making process, the Liberal Democrats' federal structure has long been regarded as a bastion of internal party democracy. With separate parties based on national regions, each one with further subdivisions, there are significant opportunities for contributions up to the Federal Policy Committee.

Can policy-making be 'too democratic'?

Some regard the Liberal Democrats' affiliative approach as problematic. Narrowing party memberships present an increasingly unrepresentative sample of the wider public — a wider public to whom parties seek to appeal in order to win seats and establish a government. For example, some policies that have been strongly supported by the Liberal Democrat membership (e.g. constitutional changes such as electoral reform and reforms to the House of Lords, and social policies such as legalising cannabis and a benevolent approach to the treatment of asylum seekers) have not played out well with the wider electorate.

National Executive Committee (NEC) The administrative head of the Labour Party coordinating policy making and candidate selection.

1922 Committee A prominent Conservative Party committee of backbenchers that liaises between the parliamentary party leaders and those MPs on the backbenches.

Structures and functions (3): leadership election

The Conservative Party

The Conservative Party had no formal mechanism for electing its leader until 1965. Between 1965 and 1997 the leadership election was restricted to the party's MPs alone. Reforms after 1997 included party members in the second stage of a ballot.

In 2005 following the resignation of Michael Howard, David Cameron and David Davis were the two strongest supported candidates by MPs. Cameron won 134,446 votes from party members (on a 78% turnout), to Davis' 64,398.

In June 2016, following David Cameron's resignation as leader of the Conservative Party (and therefore as prime minister), Theresa May announced her candidacy. May won the first round of voting a week later, receiving 165 votes from Conservative Party MPs, with rivals Andrea Leadsom receiving 66 and Michael Gove 48. The two lowest supported candidates — Liam Fox and Stephen Crabb — withdrew to back May who went on to secure 199 votes in the second round. Gove (46 votes) was duly eliminated but Leadsom (84 votes) withdrew on 1 July meaning that as the sole remaining candidate, Theresa May was declared leader of the Conservative Party without the requirement of a vote from the party membership.

The Labour Party

The Labour Party's leader was elected by the Parliamentary Labour Party for most of the twentieth century. This narrow electorate was extended and modified over the 1980s and 1990s to include union and party members while fulfilling the principle of 'one member, one vote'.

- In 2010, the weight of union influence was still felt since Ed Miliband beat his brother David despite being less supported by MPs and MEPs (46.6%) and party members (45.6%) — 59.8% of the votes of union members was sufficient to secure Ed Miliband the leadership.
- In 2015 following Ed Miliband's post-election resignation Jeremy Corbyn announced that he was to stand, ostensibly after being disillusioned at the lack of a left-wing candidate. A rule change under Miliband allowed any member of the public who supported Labour to join the party as a 'registered supporter' for £3 and qualify to participate in the leadership election. The initial outsider Corbyn was elected party leader in a landslide victory on 12 September, gaining 59.9% of first-choice votes. Corbyn's margin of victory among party members was described as the largest mandate ever won — but he remains the lowest supported leader among his own MPs.
- In 2016 Jeremy Corbyn was challenged from within his own party but was re-elected Labour leader in September with 61.8% of votes.

Structures and functions (4): candidate selection

The methods of candidate selection for the three main parties follow similar procedures. All candidates are vetted, approved and placed on a central list. When vacancies arise, local constituency parties draw up shortlists of interested applicants, all of whom must be centrally approved. Meetings and ballots then take place at a local level to determine the preferred party candidates.

Exam tip

Research the elections of Conservative and Labour leaders since 1997. Analyse and evaluate how widening the electorate may have clashed with the demands and expectations of the leadership of the parliamentary parties.

Recent candidate selection innovations have included:

- **Labour** and all women shortlists, e.g. Jacqui Smith was elected in 1997 with an all-women shortlist
- the **Conservative** Party's 'A-list'
- primary elections, e.g. Totnes in 2010

Issues and debates around party funding

Political parties play a vital role in the democratic process — at significant expense. Organisation and administration costs, not to mention election campaign spending in order to inform and educate the electorate are high. However, the steady decline of parties as mass-membership organisations has led to them seeking funds from various different sources. There are three main ways of funding political parties:

- Subscriptions from ordinary members — with declining party membership this source has dwindled in recent years.
- Donations from organisations and individuals — though this can be the source of controversy if influence or honours are felt to be 'for sale'.
- State funding — thereby ensuring that parties are not funded by wealthy individuals or groups, but could perpetuate problems of resource inequality between parties.

Recent issues and events affecting party funding have included:

- The Political Parties, Elections and Referendums Act (PPER) 2000 placed a limit of £30,000 on constituency spending and required donations of over £5,000 to be declared.
- A second PPER Act in 2009 imposed further regulations on spending by candidates in the run-up to an election, empowering the Electoral Commission to investigate cases and impose fines, restricting donations from non-UK residents, and reducing the thresholds for the declaration of donations.
- The '**loans for peerages**' scandal saw evidence that parties were getting around legislation to limit or regulate donations by accepting long-term, low-interest loans — often in return for honours in the form of peerages.
- The Philips Report of 2007 (*Strengthening Democracy: Fair and Sustainable Funding of Political Parties*) responded to concerns about the funding of political parties in order to allow them to fulfil what are widely considered valuable democratic functions. State funding, possibly based on criteria involving numbers of members, was suggested.
- Regulations have been praised for creating a new era of responsibility in electoral spending. Total spending in 2010 was less than £30 million, an amount similar to the £28.3 million spent by the Conservative Party alone in 1997. In 2015, this rose slightly to £31.5 million.

Relations with, and influence of, the media

'Managing the message' has long been a concern of political parties, especially in the age of a 24-hour news-hungry media, the internet and other informal social media platforms. This preoccupation intensified with the rise of New Labour and a realisation that the words and views of an 'off message' MP or candidate could

Knowledge check 21

Outline and explain the advantages and disadvantages of 'all-women shortlists'.

Exam tip

There are occasional examples of parties *deselecting* 'troublesome' candidates — research and explain this phenomenon.

Loans for peerages

This scandal erupted in 2006–07 when a police investigation sought to establish whether donations were procured.

have serious consequences for a party that was attempting to reassure new sections of voters of its discipline and responsibility. A number of factors have changed the impact of the media on the political agenda in recent years:

- The perceived fixation on 'managing the message' has given rise to accusations that the major parties have become more concerned with *style* — using professionals to '**spin**' a story, policy or issue favourably — than they are with the *substance* of the policies and issues themselves.

- The advance of innovative communication technology has seen the media become an increasingly *reflective* force — reinforcing the diversity and fragmentation of political views — rather than the traditional *shaping* role that had previously permitted controllers of orthodox television or print journalism to preserve their own positions and further their own agendas.

- Elected representatives, parties and governments have all engaged with the rapid expansion in communication technology in recent years to a greater or lesser extent. Interaction with 'ordinary' voters is far more immediate, and the communication and management of rapidly trending stories, issues and events far less governable than ever before.

- The phenomenon of so-called '**fake news**' mainly on social media newsfeeds, has raised further concerns about how ordinary people engage with political issues and events and how new forms of media shape the political agenda.

Factors affecting electoral outcomes

The last 40 years have been characterised by three distinct phases of national government.

1979–97

For 18 years between 1979 and 1997 the Conservative Party won four general election victories (see Table 5). In 1979, led by Margaret Thatcher, the Conservatives defeated a Labour government that was hampered by the lack of a Commons majority and by several years of industrial unrest. Thatcher campaigned on a platform of economic reform, a promise to curb the power of the unions, to create jobs and to restore Britain's place in an increasingly uncertain world.

Defeat for the Labour Party began a substantial period of opposition and transformation. Support for the Scottish National Party in 1979 collapsed as it lost 9 of its 11 MPs. The Liberal Party declined even further and Liberal leader Jeremy Thorpe lost his own North Devon seat.

In each of the following three general elections, the Conservatives secured working Commons' majorities:

- In **1983** the Conservative Party won the most decisive general election success since Labour in 1945. On the back of victory in the Falklands War, economic growth and ineffective opposition, the Conservatives added 37 seats to their 1979 total, while the Labour Party's national vote share declined by over 9%.

- In **1987** Thatcher became the first prime minister since 1820 to lead a party to three successive election victories. With the Labour Party under Neil Kinnock still some way from its move to the centre ground, the Conservative campaign

Spin A term used to describe efforts of party leaders to gain favourable coverage by carefully managing the presentation of policies to the media.

Fake news
Uncorroborated news stories, usually on informal social media platforms, that appear to many to be indistinguishable from news reported by 'reputable' news channels.

Exam tip

Ensure that you are aware of the overlap with the role of the media in influencing electoral outcomes which features in the topic on elections.

successfully focused on economic stability. It withstood a 1.5% swing towards Labour and secured a government majority of more than 100 seats.

- In **1992** the Conservatives won a fourth successive election victory. This time under the leadership of John Major who had replaced the ousted Thatcher as leader and prime minister in 1990. The success was unexpected since opinion polls had consistently predicted a Labour win. However, the governing majority was slashed to a precarious 21 seats.

Table 5 Conservative Party election victories, 1979–92

	National vote (%)	Seats won	Majority
1979	43.9	339	43
1983	42.4	397	144
1987	42.2	376	102
1992	41.4	336	21

1997–2010

A succession of by-election defeats running up to 1997 had entirely eroded the Conservative Party's majority and against a backdrop of 'Tory **sleaze**', disunity over Europe, and declining economic credibility following **Black Wednesday**, the party plunged to its worst electoral defeat since 1906, returning just 165 MPs. The Labour Party's rejuvenation under Tony Blair was complete as a 10.2% swing from Conservative to Labour saw it win 418 seats and establish its largest ever parliamentary majority (see Table 6). Victories were also gained in the next two general elections:

- In **2001** the Labour Party continued to profit from weak Conservative opposition as William Hague failed to make inroads. Despite a record low turnout of just 59.4%, the Labour Party retained an overwhelming majority.
- In **2005** despite Tony Blair's decline in popularity since the Iraq War, the Labour Party won again in what was to be Blair's last election as leader. Its vote share of just 35.2% was the lowest polled by any majority-forming government in British history.

Table 6 Labour Party election victories, 1997–2005

	National vote (%)	Seats won	Majority
1997	43.2	418	179
2001	40.7	413	167
2005	35.2	355	66

2010–present

Gordon Brown's reluctance to call an immediate general election upon his accession — and relative popularity — in 2007 proved his undoing as a resurgent Conservative Party under David Cameron in **2010** won the largest number of votes

Sleaze A series of scandals and disreputable behaviour among Conservative MPs in the 1990s — notably taking cash for asking questions in Parliament — substantially undermined trust in politicians.

Black Wednesday On 16 September 1992 the falling pound forced the UK out of the European Exchange Rate Mechanism and undermined the Conservative Party's reputation for economic competence.

and seats. However, the Conservatives were 20 seats short of a Commons majority and needed to form a coalition government with the Liberal Democrats. In securing over 6.8 million votes (23%), the Liberal Democrats considered themselves to be worthy coalition partners and the 2010 election was notable for showing signs that voters were prepared to seek alternatives to the two main parties, who polled less than two-thirds of the national vote for the first time in modern electoral history (see Table 7).

The **2015** general election was remarkable for several reasons:

- Opinion polls had consistently predicted a hung parliament but the Conservatives won an unexpected majority with 330 seats.
- The Labour Party had a disastrous election, losing 24 seats and failing to mount a credible challenge to the Conservatives.
- The SNP had been growing in popularity, but on the back of a surge in support following 2014's 'No' vote in the Scottish independence referendum, won 56 of the 59 Scottish parliamentary seats to become the third biggest party in the Commons.
- The Liberal Democrats experienced their worst electoral outcome since their formation, losing all but eight of their parliamentary seats.
- UKIP outstripped Liberal Democrat support, with over 3.5 million votes, yet returned just one MP.

The **2017** general election was arguably even more remarkable:

- Opinion polls just prior to the calling of the snap election were particularly favourable to the Conservatives — some indicated a 20-point lead and a landslide victory.
- In the event, the Conservative parliamentary majority was wiped out (despite polling over 42% of the vote) and the Labour Party gained 30 seats.
- An election that was called to strengthen the Brexit negotiating hand of Theresa May's 'strong and stable' leadership proved anything but, and the prime minister's own position was seriously compromised.
- The surge in support for Jeremy Corbyn's leadership, while not electorally decisive, profoundly changed media attitudes, and those of many MPs within his own party.
- The SNP's focus on Scottish independence was neutralised by the loss of 21 seats and nearly a million votes.
- UKIP were all but wiped out as an electoral force, receiving just 594,068 votes (1.8%) and losing their one MP.

Table 7 Conservative Party election results, 2010, 2015 and 2017

	National vote (%)	Seats won	Majority
2010	36.1	306	−20
2015	36.8	330	12
2017	42.4	318	−6

Policies of minor parties and their impact on political debates and the political agenda

Nationalist parties and their impact

The Scottish National Party (SNP)

Supporting devolution in 1997, the SNP went from minor party in the 1980s to a nationalist party with major political significance, forming a single-party majority government in the Scottish Parliament following the 2011 election. However, it fell two seats short of a majority when it lost six seats in the 2016 election.

■ The SNP-backed campaign for independence was dealt a substantial blow when the Scottish referendum returned a 'No' vote based on 55% of the electorate in 2014.

■ A significant response to the referendum result was a surge in SNP membership. On the day of the independence referendum in October 2014, membership stood at 25,642. Within 6 months this had risen to over 100,000.

■ In the 2015 general election, 56 of the 59 Scottish constituencies were won by the SNP making it the third largest party in Parliament. This presence made it a credible threat to government policy in areas that affect the regions such as international relations and the economy.

■ However, the Scottish Conservatives had a resurgence in 2017 under leader Ruth Davidson. With just one seat from 2015, the 13 seats they emerged with — at the expense of the SNP who were reduced to 34 seats — was their best performance north of the border since 1983.

Plaid Cymru (PC)

Appetite for regional government in Wales has historically been less prominent than that in Scotland, exemplified by the 50.3% 'Yes' vote in 1997 which supported the creation of the Welsh Assembly, from a 50.1% turnout. Plaid Cymru formed part of a coalition government with the Welsh Labour Party from 2007 but support declined at the polls in 2011. In 2016 it won 12 of the 60 seats available with Labour winning 29.

One major recent change has been the devolution of further primary legislative powers to the Welsh Assembly. A 2011 referendum question asked: 'Do you want the Assembly now to be able to make laws on all matters in the 20 subject areas it has powers for?' A majority of 63.5% voted 'Yes' and the Welsh Assembly now has full legislative competence in areas as diverse as health, education, housing and tourism.

Legislative competence
The ability for bodies beneath Parliament to pass Acts in legally designated areas. For the Welsh Assembly these are detailed in Schedule 5 of the Government of Wales Act 2006.

Northern Ireland

Party politics in Northern Ireland is based on many decades of political and religious violence, primarily about the status of the province with regard to the rest of the UK and the Republic of Ireland. The Good Friday Agreement (1998) paved the way for Northern Ireland to become a self-governing territory with its own assembly and executive. Party divisions remain on religious or sectarian lines and while a range of parties hold seats in the assembly, the two main political parties are as follows.

- The Democratic Unionist Party (DUP) has strong links with Protestant institutions and voters and former ties to loyalist paramilitary groups such as the Ulster Volunteer Force (UVF) and the Ulster Defence Association (UDA)/Ulster Freedom Fighters (UFF). It currently holds 28 of the 90 seats in the assembly. Its 10-seat haul in the 2017 UK general election put it in prime position to offer support to the Conservative minority government.
- Sinn Fein holds 27 seats in the assembly. Its background is Catholic and the party has historically had links with the Provisional IRA.

The main impact of Northern Ireland party politics is that the proportional electoral system used routinely results in fragile coalitions between parties that have a long history of suspicion and animosity. While there have been periods of stability — and the post-1998 period is one of remarkable peace and calm compared to the conflict and bloodshed in the preceding years— devolved institutions have had to be suspended at times, with power reverting to Westminster.

Minor parties and their impact

UK Independence Party (UKIP)

UKIP's profile rose dramatically with 16.5% of the vote at the 2009 European elections securing it 13 seats. Its vocal leader Nigel Farage captured many disenchanted eurosceptic Tory voters as well as those who felt that the main political parties do not offer sufficient direction in tackling key issues of immigration and law and order. Its second place (27.8%) in the Eastleigh parliamentary by-election in 2013 was dismissed by some as a protest vote but the party's prominence continued to rise:

- In the first time that a political party other than the Labour Party or Conservative Party won the popular vote in a British election since the 1906 general election, UKIP topped the 2014 European elections, winning 26.6% of the national vote and 24 seats overall — from every region apart from Northern Ireland.
- In the 2015 general election, UKIP polled over 3.8 million votes (12.7%). While the party only won one seat, the impact of its vote was at the expense of the Labour and Liberal Democrat parties in many marginal constituencies.
- UKIP's attraction was a major feature in the referendum vote to leave the EU. The party attracted significant support and funds and in June 2016 52% of voters voted in favour of 'Brexit', but its vote share had dwindled to under 600,000 votes in the 2017 general election (1.8%).

The Green Party

The Greens secured modest representation in recent European elections but broke through in 2010 by winning a Westminster seat for the first time — Brighton Pavilion with 31.3% of the vote. With other parties embracing a green agenda, its share of the national vote in 2010 stuck around 1%. In both 2015 and 2017, the party retained its one seat, but its vote share went up to 1.15 million voters in 2015 and back down to 525,371 in 2017.

Exam tip

Remember that the impact of devolution — on policy, multi-party politics and government relations — overlaps with the devolution topic.

Knowledge check 22

Briefly explain the impact of UKIP on party politics in the 2015 general election.

Development towards a multi-party system in the UK and its impact on government and policy

The traditional two-party system in the UK

Traditional views of party politics in the UK stress the predominance of Labour and Conservatives within a two-party system. Based on seats won and governments formed this view is difficult to dispute. But the introduction of alternative electoral systems has seen patterns of representation change at different electoral levels.

Other types of party system

One-party systems

States with a constitutionally proscribed ruling party (e.g. Cuba or North Korea) or states which see opposition party support restricted or intimidated (e.g. Zimbabwe).

Dominant-party systems

Different from one-party systems, a natural or organic dominance of the political system by one party (e.g. India or Japan).

Multi-party systems

A larger number of parties play a significant role in political life — gaining representation and governing responsibility (e.g. Germany).

Debate: does the UK still have a two-party system?

Yes:

■ One of the main strengths of the FPTP system is its creation of a strong single-party government in all but two of the post-war general elections, all of which were won by the Labour or the Conservative parties.

■ The system invariably over-rewards opposition parties and Labour currently holds 39% of the seats from 29% of the national vote.

■ The two main parties have never held less than 85% of the seats in the House of Commons.

No:

■ Vote shares of the two main parties in general elections have declined from around 95% in the 1950s to 65% in 2010.

■ Recent decades have hardly been characterised by regular to-and-fro between two parties. The 1979–97 period was dominated by the Conservatives and 1997–2010 dominated by Labour.

■ In the regions and when alternative systems are used, nationalist parties and independents do far better — the Scottish National Party have formed a single-party government north of the border and UKIP, the Green Party and the BNP all gained seats in the 2009 European Parliament election.

Knowledge check 23

What is the difference between a one-party system and a dominant party system?

Exam tip

Make sure you differentiate between electoral outcomes in the regions and in Westminster when considering whether the UK is a multi-party system.

Summary

After studying this topic you should be able to:

- Define a political party and distinguish between different functions and roles using contemporary examples.
- Understand and evaluate the various ideological traditions and developments of the main parties.
- Contrast current party policies with long-standing ideological trends within and between the main parties, in order to evaluate the extent to which the modern parties have deviated from their ideological roots.

- Understand how UK parties are organised, how they select leaders and candidates and how they formulate party policy.
- Evaluate the strengths and impact of minor parties in the UK — and the various roles played by them.

Pressure groups

Pressure groups and democracy: pluralism

A pressure group is most accurately described as an organised, often single-issue group with a membership that shares common interests or aims. Pressure groups do not tend to field candidates for election but instead seek to influence government policy or legislation. They are referred to in different ways — as 'interest groups', 'lobby groups' or 'cause groups' — and include trade unions (e.g. **Unison**, the second largest union) who seek to advance the interests of the sections of society that they represent. Other groups may seek to promote a particular cause or issue (e.g. Friends of the Earth and environmental issues). The very existence of pressure groups is seen by many as a vital feature of a tolerant democracy.

What are the main functions of pressure groups?

Five key roles that pressure groups play can be summarised as:

- encouraging public participation in the political arena by offering legitimate and effective opportunities to challenge government activity
- providing essential channels of communication between the government and the governed
- protecting minority rights, e.g. Shelter and the homeless
- providing expert information to the government, e.g. the Automobile Association on transport issues
- mobilising public support for certain issues that may include the use of direct action tactics, e.g. the 2010 student protests against the rise in tuition fees.

What is pluralism?

Pluralism is a theory of political interaction that provides a basis for understanding how governments and groups interact in the decision-making process. Pluralist theories emphasise that decision-making power is widely and evenly spread across

Unison has 1.3 million members who work in local authorities; the NHS; police and justice; universities, colleges and schools; the electricity and gas industries; the water industry; the Environment Agency; transport; and the community and voluntary sector.

society, and that many different groups and organisations — including charities, universities, consumer groups, trade unions, faiths and private business — challenge and debate with each other in a healthy and positive way, thereby strengthening the democratic process. Needless to say, pluralists view the existence of pressure groups as both positive and indispensable, and stress a number of features within democracies:

- With the many countervailing influences and pressures within pluralist societies, no single group can achieve dominance. Pluralism stands in opposition to theories stressing that decision-making power is concentrated in the hands of a small few (or a 'power elite').
- While resources vary from one group to another, the free and wide access to, for example, growing a membership or accumulating wealth through donations, means that groups have fair opportunities to further their aims and exert influence.
- By joining together to form groups, citizens are represented far more effectively than they would be on their own.

Pluralist societies are therefore ones in which participation in political life is not just reserved to voting in elections. Instead, decisions are competed over by different groups that aim to negotiate with and persuade those in power — good policy is therefore the result of social pressure. It would be fair for larger, well-supported groups to have a greater 'say' but only as long as minority groups are not left out. It is the responsibility of the government to mediate between groups and ensure that all appropriate views and parts of society are accounted for.

Is the UK a 'pluralist democracy'?

While the UK exhibits many features of a **pluralist democracy**, it would be difficult to argue that it satisfies the criteria entirely. Four ways that the UK could be considered to be a pluralist democracy are:

- Important decisions that affect citizens' lives are made on multiple levels — local, regional and national.
- Elections are held regularly and see a wide range of parties competing for elected office. Elections themselves are conducted under secret ballot with universal suffrage.
- A huge range of pressure groups exist, representing a diverse array of causes and interests.
- Rights and liberties — especially in the context of free speech, assembly and association and the right to protest — are protected under the rule of law.

Four ways that the UK does not entirely satisfy the criteria of pluralist democracy are:

- UK-wide elections are carried out under the majoritarian system of first past the post, meaning that votes to seats ratios are distorted. Many voting groups within society are under-represented or not represented at all within the UK Parliament.
- Parliament, with its unelected second chamber, uneven relationships between government branches, and a lack of separation of powers that allows the executive to dominate the legislature, provides grounds for significant criticisms.

Pluralist democracy A system of government which enables and encourages participation and allows for free and fair competition between multiple completing interests.

■ Political engagement is often characterised by apathy and disillusionment — turnout at elections is low, as is the membership of the political parties that vie for power.
■ The UK lacks a codified constitution to limit government, and to set out and protect rights and liberties.

In terms of political decision making, the steady transfer of power to unelected bodies in the UK — in recent years to regional development agencies, quangos, free-standing agencies, and regulatory bodies such as Ofcom, and Ofsted — has undermined the argument that the UK is a pluralist democracy in which multiple groups have the ability to exert genuine pressure on the decision-making process.

Do pressure groups promote democracy?

In order to analyse and evaluate whether pressure groups promote, help or hinder the democratic process, a contextual definition of 'democracy' is important to measure pressure groups activity against. Within the context of a study of pressure groups, a 'pluralist democracy' might be considered to include:

■ a well-educated citizenry, empowered to participate in the shaping of policy in important areas
■ a wide dispersal of power among healthily competing (pressuring) groups in a political system that is not dominated by elites
■ a responsive government that respects the rights of citizens to have their say within the democratic principles of the state.

Factors which suggest that pressure groups promote democracy

Enhancing and supplementing representation

A significant strength of pressure groups is that they can 'bridge the gap' by representing citizens between more formal but less frequent democratic opportunities, such as elections. In almost every area of our lives, there are groups working to secure favourable legislation, to avoid unfavourable legislation, to highlight concerns or to engage the wider public. Whether as students, parents, renters, homeowners, holiday-makers, motorists, walkers, conservationists, sports enthusiasts or library-goers, there are groups to represent our interests to those that govern us.

Encouraging participation

One of the primary collective functions of pressure groups is to engage citizens in a way that ensures that governments do not become dictatorial. An active and well-informed citizenry is the best way to prevent the excessive accumulation of power in the hands of a governing elite, and to ensure that decision makers remain responsive and accountable. With party memberships falling and turnout at elections variable, pressure groups have increasingly plugged the 'democratic deficit'. Their focus on a narrow range of issues (often single issues) and their encouragement for individuals to participate actively in furthering causes or raising awareness has attracted many individuals — especially young people — otherwise disillusioned with mainstream politics.

Knowledge check 24

What is a quango? How has the rise of quangos contributed to the undermining of democratic processes in the UK?

Exam tip

Make sure that you understand the term 'pluralist democracy' and the conditions for it to exist.

Education and expertise

The educative value of pressure groups for the democratic process is twofold. First, pressure groups provide a significant amount of information to the public, thereby contributing towards a better-informed and better-educated electorate. Pressure groups are, by definition, autonomous of government so they provide important independent messages to promote political debate and discussion. Second, one of the most important functions of pressure groups is the expert knowledge that they provide to the government. Many pressure groups are able to develop an expertise in their field, generating new ideas, solutions, or programmes of reform, which elected officials do not have the time or knowledge to develop for themselves.

Protecting minorities

Many might consider this to be the most significant strength of pressure groups: that of ensuring that all groups within society — especially ones less able to further their own causes, such as the disabled, children or animals — are protected and afforded equal status. Without pressure groups performing this vital democratic function, the nineteenth-century liberal philosopher John Stuart Mill's warning of the **tyranny of the majority** could well come true. Political parties will inevitably seek majority support, thereby ignoring the interests of many minorities. It is pressure groups that perform the vital function of ensuring that party rule does not become tyranny.

Undemocratic features of pressure groups

Inequality of influence

One of the key criticisms of pressure groups is that they do not operate within a pluralist democracy. Instead, pressure groups serve to entrench existing divisions and allow the powerful to accumulate even more power. Groups do not enjoy the amount of influence that their size and support warrants and some groups wield disproportionate power. This may be down to the strategically important position that some groups hold within society (e.g. doctors or farmers) or their wealth or privileged links with the decision makers. Conversely, other groups may well experience a disproportionately lower level of influence (e.g. the unemployed, prisoners, the homeless) meaning that far from promoting democracy, pressure groups undermine it.

Inequality of resources

Alongside unequal influence, one of the biggest criticisms of pressure group activity is that it vastly favours groups with better access to wealth. Groups that represent large sectional interests invariably have the wealth to sustain a permanent workforce and to mount impressive campaigns — this does not necessarily mean that their causes or interests are of more social or democratic benefit than groups that rely on modest donations from the public. Similarly, well-supported groups can have a disproportionate influence on governments that understandably do not want to alienate significant blocks of voters. The high election turnouts among elderly voters have led many to conclude that issues which disproportionately affect them (e.g. pensions and healthcare) have been protected in contrast to issues that affect younger people or non-voters (e.g. university tuition fees, secondary education and low-waged employment rights).

Tyranny of the majority
The fundamental weakness of democracy — that just because a majority of people vote for something (in the case of the 2016 EU referendum, 52%) it does not necessarily mean that it is 'right'.

Internal democracy of pressure groups

Critics of pressure group influence highlight concerns over the basis of their power. Unlike parties, most pressure groups are not transparent, accountable organisations: their leaders are rarely elected and are not generally publicly accountable; policies can be arrived at with little recourse to wider members. There is a growing trend for groups to be run by highly paid 'professionals' with personal career objectives that may not align with those of the group's membership. The BMA, for example, was forced to cancel strike plans over junior doctors' contracts after its members highlighted concerns for patient safety.

Undermining the democratic process

There are a number of further factors to consider in the debate over whether pressure groups undermine democracy. These include the fact that much effective pressure group activity goes on 'behind closed doors', making objective scrutiny of the process of policy formulation and decision making very difficult. Additionally, there has been a significant growth in direct action tactics — civil disobedience, blockades or media stunts — that can intimidate or inconvenience and also undermine the constitutional framework of the state. Finally, taking account of all opinions in an increasingly fragmented or 'hyper-pluralist' state can be a costly and inefficient environment in which to create sensible policies.

Political scientist E. E. Schattschneider is often quoted in the context of pressure groups and democracy, stating that 'the flaw in the pluralist heaven is that the heavenly choir sings with a strong upper-class accent'. For critics of pressure group activity the increasingly narrow self-interest of many groups, alongside the disproportionate impact of middle-class groups in promoting or defending their interests and dominating the **political agenda**, mean that pressure groups make it more difficult for governments to formulate and pursue policies that are in the long-term interests of larger society.

Other influences on government and Parliament

Think tanks

Think tanks have been around for many centuries and it is estimated that up to 7,000 currently exist worldwide. Think tanks are usually non-profit or charitable organisations whose objectives are to research areas of particular interest — usually in political, economic, military, social or cultural spheres — and **advocate** on behalf of supportive individuals, groups and organisations. The most significant and influential think tanks in the UK tend to exist as public policy institutes, operating independently of government (many stress their non-affiliated or non-partisan credentials), seeking to shape policy according to their own political perspectives or leanings (see Table 8).

Political agenda This refers to the prevailing or dominant issues that concern government and society at any given time.

Knowledge check 25

Outline and explain how pressure groups protect minority interests.

Exam tip

Research and develop the issue of internal pressure group democracy when considering the debate over pressure groups and democracy.

Think tank Usually a public policy institute that researches significant issues and seeks to advise the government accordingly.

Advocate Supporting and enabling people to express their views on a cause or policy.

Table 8 Influential think tanks in the UK

Institute of Public Policy Research (IPPR)	A left-wing think tank that publishes around 50 reports a year, mainly on economic and social matters. The IPPR has been particularly successful in campaigning on issues that affect the north — especially driving the Northern Powerhouse agenda.
Demos	A cross-party think tank dedicated to evidence-based solutions to issues involving education and skills, health and housing. Recent projects include the 2015 'Tune In, Turn Out' campaign to encourage young people to vote.
Civitas (The Institute for the Study of Civil Society)	A non-partisan think tank — though described as 'right of centre' in media circles — aiming to promote better understanding of issues affecting families, health and crime. In 2017 it campaigned for a new inspectorate to replace Ofsted for free schools and academies.
Policy Exchange	Referred to by the *Daily Telegraph* as 'the largest [and] most influential think tank on the right', Policy Exchange reports on matters such as health, education and energy and has influenced government policy on housing.
Centre for Social Justice (CSJ)	Established as an independent think tank in 2004 with the aim of putting social justice at the heart of British politics. It is said to be one of the most influential think tanks among Theresa May's advisors.
Fabian Society	A socialist think tank that provided the intellectual roots for the modern Labour Party. It heavily influenced the Labour government in the 1990s and 2000s on matters including tax reforms and health spending.

Lobbyists

The term 'lobbying' has its origins in opportunistic meetings with MPs and peers in the Palace of Westminster's halls or lobbies between debates and votes. Such opportunities provide chances to further causes or seek support.

Lobbying can occur on an individual or group level, taking the 'traditional' form of letters written to elected representatives or visits to the Palace of Westminster. However, most lobbying is now carried out in a professional capacity through lobby firms (see Table 9).

Lobby firms employ well-connected individuals — invariably those currently serving as MPs and peers or ex-MPs, local authority councillors and public affairs experts — to use their contacts with decision makers to raise issues on behalf of fee-paying clients. For some groups, the routine use of lobby firms can ensure that their issues remain on the political agenda.

The practice of lobbying has long prompted concerns — in particular the direct and lucrative route that some MPs take into lobbying immediately after leaving public office. The House of Commons Public Administration Select Committee published a 2009 report entitled 'Lobbying: Access and Influence in Whitehall' which attempted to balance the legitimacy of lobbying in a democratic country with the potentially corrupting effect of a lack of effective regulation.

The industry remained largely self-regulated until recently, but the Transparency of Lobbying, Non-Party Campaigning and Trade Union Act which came into force in 2015 requires that all professional lobbyists are listed on the register of consultant lobbyists.

Table 9 Major lobby firms operating in the UK

Burson-Marsteller	A global public relations company founded in 1953 and operating in 98 countries worldwide. Conservative former minister Andrew MacKay joined the firm in 2010 as an international consultant immediately after stepping down as an MP following the expenses scandal.
PLMR (Political Lobbying and Media Relations)	A lobbying firm with clients that include global businesses, such as SKY and BAE Systems, universities and charities. The company has raised awareness for Combat Stress and campaigned for standardised cigarette packages on behalf of Cancer Research UK.

Corporations

Businesses with significant investment in the UK and large UK-based workforces can have substantial influence over policy and legislation. Supermarket chains such as Tesco (519,000 employees) and Sainsbury's (150,000 employees), pharmaceutical companies like GlaxoSmithKline (worth over £65 billion) and AstraZeneca (worth over £50 billion), and car manufacturing groups such as Toyota and Nissan, with workforces of many thousands in politically sensitive areas of the UK, are involved in formulating policies related to, for example, business regulation, enterprise initiatives and taxation. Major companies all have expert policy units that scrutinise favourable or unfavourable legislation, and representatives who will meet frequently with government officials.

Businesses or corporations that organise themselves into coherent '**federations**', united for the purposes of furthering their collective interests, can have a particularly significant influence (see Table 10).

Federation Within the context of pressure group activity this refers to a number of groups joining together to enhance their collective pressure.

Table 10 Federations of businesses and industries

UK Finance	After a merger of six financial trade associations, including the British Bankers Association (BBA), in 2016, UK Finance represents nearly 300 of the leading firms providing finance, banking, markets and payments-related services in or from the UK.
Confederation of British Industry (CBI)	The CBI represents 190,000 businesses that employ over 7 million people, including the 55,000 members of the National Farmers' Union. The CBI styles itself as 'the voice of business' and aims to promote the conditions in which businesses of all sizes can prosper. In September 2014 the CBI started *The Great Business Debate* to increase public confidence in business. It was embroiled in controversy in 2014 after publicly backing the campaign against Scottish independence, contrary to the position of many of its members.

Media

Since the turn of the century, the transformation in opportunities presented by the rapid shift from the established 'old' media of print journalism and terrestrial television channels, to the 'new' media of 24-hour news, swift advances in information and communication technology and multiple social media platforms, has had a dramatic impact on pressure groups' activity.

Until recently, pressure groups' media tactics tended to revolve around whole-page advertisements in the national press, orthodox press releases or the production of television advertisements. The expense of a coordinated 'traditional' media campaign usually meant that only well-supported or well-established groups could engage. For example, in 2005 the NSPCC spent £3 million on television advertising for its hard-hitting Full Stop campaign to raise awareness of violence against children.

Most established charities still spend significant sums on maintaining or advancing their profile through multi-media channels. In 2015 it was revealed that Save the Children paid over £700,000 in 2014 to a single advertising agency to promote its image and campaigns.

However, the rise of alternative media platforms, social networking sites and smartphones has opened up the media to groups big and small. Creative and imaginative campaigns are communicated at little cost. **Trending** — often using Twitter hashtags — has seen issues rise up the political agenda at great speed. Groups encouraging anti-discrimination, pro-immigration, celebrating diversity or campaigning for justice or gender equality have used new media platforms to engage young, politically conscious tech-savvy supporters.

Typologies of pressure groups

Classification by aims (sectional and cause)

A traditional way of classifying pressure groups is by aim, purpose or goal.

Sectional groups

Sectional groups seek to advance the common interests of a particular section of society, e.g. nurses, transport workers, ethnic groups or policemen. They are sometimes criticised for being self-interested — motivated by the economic advancement of their members rather than for the benefit of the wider community. **Peak groups** combine organisations with a common interest and can be particularly powerful.

The **Trades Union Congress** (TUC) is good example of a sectional 'peak' group. It is a federation of trade unions in England and Wales, representing over 50 trade unions with a combined total of nearly 6 million members. It was founded in 1868 and continues to campaign for trade union aims and values. In recent years it has influenced the pay and conditions of young workers and in September 2016 the TUC forced Sports Direct to undergo an independent review into its treatment of workers.

Cause groups

Cause groups seek to promote a specific set of objectives, not necessarily of direct or immediate benefit to their members. Also referred to as 'attitudinal' or 'issue' groups they may have a specific cause in mind, such as Plane Stupid that seeks to counteract aviation expansion, or be more general in focus, such as reducing poverty or advancing human rights.

Trending Most associated with Twitter, trending refers to a surge in support or interest in a particular issue or topic.

Knowledge check 26

Explain why lobbying could be a strength and a weakness within a democracy.

Exam tip

Ensure that your responses include recent examples of how groups have *actually influenced* government and Parliament.

Peak group An umbrella pressure group that speaks on behalf of a number of groups with a common interest.

A well-established cause group is **Friends of the Earth**, an organisation that has sought to find solutions to environmental problems for over 40 years. It has successfully campaigned to protect conservation areas, to promote sustainability and recycling, and to highlight significant issues such as the decline in the bee population, flood defences and air pollution.

Problems with the 'sectional or cause' typology

The boundary between sectional and cause groups has become increasingly blurred leading to criticism of the classification:

■ Many sectional groups style themselves as cause groups in order to promote the wider, moral benefits of their interests. The National Union of Teachers campaigns for educational values in general, while seeking to improve the economic interests of its members.

■ Many groups now have sectional *and* cause characteristics. Shelter may not directly enhance the lives of people who have homes, but living in a society which cares for homeless people is of general benefit.

Classification by status (insider and outsider)

In the 1990s political scientist Wynn Grant advanced a way of classifying pressure groups that emphasised status with regard to the decision makers as the key factor in understanding the differences between groups — and why some were more successful than others.

Insider groups

Insider groups have significant access to decision makers and core insiders (e.g. the British Medical Association) play a key role in formulating policy. Other groups range from specialist insiders who play a major role in specific areas (e.g. the Automobile Association), to peripheral insiders who only feature occasionally (e.g. Addaction, a drug and alcohol treatment charity), to prisoner groups who are effectively part of the government (e.g. the Commission for Racial Equality).

Some pressure groups are so close to decision makers that they have permanent seats on government policy committees and agencies, finding themselves at the centre of the decision-making process. The National Farmers' Union is a typical example. It is advantageous to government that all agricultural policy should be considered by representatives of the farming community at an early stage, as they will have to conform to these policies.

Outsider groups

Outsider groups range from ideological outsiders, who deliberately position themselves outside mainstream politics (e.g. Greenpeace or Amnesty International), to outsiders by necessity whose chosen methods mean they will never be actively consulted (e.g. Fathers4Justice). Outsider groups also feature 'potential' or 'aspiring' insiders, who might be awaiting a more favourable political climate.

The Centre for Policy Studies (CPS) was very much in favour in the 1970s and 1980s, generating a wealth of reports and research — on free market economics, enterprise and social responsibility. Since Margaret Thatcher and Keith Joseph founded the CPS in 1974, its perspectives and proposals were well aligned to the Conservative

Exam tip

Ensure that you are aware of the subdivisions within the sectional and cause typology.

government of the 1980s. While the group fell out of favour in the 1990s and 2000s, it is experiencing a resurgence amid more favourable political conditions under Theresa May.

Problems with the 'insider or outsider' typology

Difficulties associated with classifying groups according to their status:

- Some studies estimate that over 90% of groups have some level of 'inside access', since government bodies consult with a very wide range of groups.
- Most outsider groups were seen as having to resort to outsider tactics after failing to achieve insider status, but a large number of high-profile groups (e.g. Live8 and Friends of the Earth) have advanced their causes without insider status.

A key development in pressure group activity, especially since the 1980s, has been the growth of groups that defy classification (whether by aims or by status) by spanning social and economic divides in support of large-scale social movements or causes. These are most unlike traditional pressure groups, having no formal membership and often arising rapidly or spontaneously around issues such as poverty, anti-capitalism, environmental or narrow social issues. Their methods are far more likely to include **direct action**, bypassing conventional methods and adopting confrontational tactics such as sit-ins, demonstrations and sometimes illegal acts. Examples include:

- protests against fuel tax rises in 2000
- anti-Iraq war demonstrations in 2003
- anti-poverty Live8 concerts and rallies in 2005
- university tuition fees protests in 2010
- protests against welfare cuts 2016

Direct action This refers to forms of protest involving degrees of civil disobedience, illegality or even violence.

Knowledge check 27

Identify and explain two main problems with the insider and outsider typology.

Pressure group detailed studies: in, out or in-between?

Many of the most successful groups run 'mixed method' campaigns that combine traditional, high-level meetings with key decision makers alongside elements of direct action to engage the public and generate media coverage. The vast majority of groups — estimated at more than 90% — have some kind of 'inside track' to the decision makers. While this might support arguments that the UK is a pluralist democracy, consultation may not often lead to success.

More insider than outsider

The Howard League for Penal Reform

The Howard League (www.howardleague.org) has been campaigning for prison reform for over 150 years. Funded by charitable trusts and from the subscriptions of its 12,000 members, the group is a national charity working for a reduction in crime and offending, and fewer people in prison.

The group runs low-profile campaigns directed at decision makers — such as its '3 Rs of Prison Reform' that aims to reduce the prison population and support prison staff. Alongside these are more high-profile public campaigns such as Books for Prisoners. The Books for Prisoners campaign was a response to the justice secretary 'clamping down' on prisoner perks by banning the sending in of books to prisoners from friends and family in 2013. The Howard League used direct action tactics, which included Poet Laureate Carol Ann Duffy reading outside Pentonville Prison and prominent letters to the *Daily Telegraph* signed by hundreds of well-known authors, to reverse the government's policy decision within months.

The Howard League was particularly successful in its campaign against the introduction of the criminal courts charge in 2015, which required a mandatory fine (of up to £1,200) to be charged to everyone convicted of an offence regardless of his or her ability to pay. By compiling a dossier of unfair cases and presenting them to the media and to the justice secretary, the group was successful in abolishing the criminal courts charge within 5 months.

Although the Howard League is frequently engaged with key decision makers within the Department of Justice, the prison population has more than doubled over the last two decades in defiance of the group's activities to focus greater attention and resources on programmes that tackle the causes of crime — especially mental health, drink and drugs addiction, and abuse.

Cruelty Free International

Cruelty Free (www.crueltyfreeinternational.org) is a UK-based organisation working to end animal experiments worldwide. It is the most influential single-issue group campaigning against animal testing for cosmetics and for medical experimentation. Although relatively small — it has under 20 employees — the group's substantial legal and medical expertise means that its reach is considerable, and that key decision makers on a national, European and international level have consulted the group on policy and legislation.

Major recent successes and ongoing campaigns include:

- The group's 'Leaping Bunny' logo certifying that a product is 'cruelty free' has been adopted by over 600 companies and brands, allowing shoppers to choose products not tested on animals.
- The group was at the vanguard of the campaign that resulted in the EU adopting an animal-tested cosmetics ban that came into force in 2013. Cruelty Free's policy team negotiated with key decision makers at EU level.
- In 2015 it was granted permission to take the Home Office to court. The group sought to bring a judicial review against the government department for violating EU animal experiments regulations.
- However, 80% of countries still permit cosmetics testing on animals. Cruelty Free is aiming for a global animal-tested cosmetics ban, lobbying the United Nations to adopt an international convention to end animal testing for cosmetics worldwide.

The group is independent of government, funded from public donations.

More outsider than insider

The Campaign for Nuclear Disarmament (CND)

CND (www.cnduk.org) is a group that campaigns for unilateral nuclear disarmament in the UK and multilateral nuclear disarmament worldwide. It opposes all forms of military action involving nuclear, chemical and biological warfare and the building of nuclear power stations in the UK. The group was formed in 1957 and styles itself as Europe's largest single-issue peace campaign.

CND is notable for its longevity — considering many cause groups have short life spans — and for its prominent role as a campaigning group in the UK's political culture. In the 1950s and 1960s, the CND-organised Aldermaston marches attracted tens of thousands of demonstrators at their peak; in the 1980s with the Cold War at its height, the group claimed to have over 250,000 members. When Cruise missiles were deployed in the UK in 1983 over 300,000 marched in protest in London.

Despite its outsider/direct action tactics, CND has maintained a relationship with the Labour Party over several decades. The group claims to have significantly influenced the party in the direction of unilateral nuclear disarmament in the 1960s and 1980s. In 2015 long-time supporter of CND Jeremy Corbyn was elected leader of the Labour Party — although party policy did not change to embrace nuclear disarmament and, disappointingly for CND, Corbyn did not oppose the renewal of the UK's Trident nuclear deterrent in 2016. However, the Labour leader began to renew his commitment to a nuclear free UK in the 2017 general election campaign.

UK Uncut

UK Uncut (www.ukuncut.org.uk) is a grassroots movement that predominantly uses civil disobedience to oppose government cuts to public services and to highlight exploitative corporations.

Despite its first organised protest only occurring in 2010, UK Uncut has risen to prominence with its many stunts and media campaigns. It has closed down stores such as Vodafone and Fortnum & Mason with sit-down protests, blockaded Westminster Bridge and Oxford Circus, and led the campaign to force corporations like Starbucks to pay what the group considers to be a fair share of tax.

UK Uncut has also worked with the 'establishment' to pursue its aims. The group campaigns prominently against corporate tax avoidance and has found support among top lawyers, tax experts and MPs in its bid to reform corporation tax and close loopholes that, in its view, have allowed companies to avoid paying tax. However, in 2013 the group failed in the High Court to overturn the settlement agreement between the HMRC and Goldman Sachs investment bank.

Methods used by pressure groups

The methods employed by pressure groups to achieve their aims vary greatly and depend largely upon the group's objectives and their status with regard to key decision-makers. Regardless of the erosion of typologies such as insider and outsider, groups that aim to cultivate even moderate relationships with decision-makers will have to act within the law and within the constitutional framework of the state. In addition, it is worth remembering that many groups' objectives are local – possibly focusing on planning issues or changes in the provision of local services such as transport routes, libraries or other amenities – and do not require any level of engagement with central government.

Identifying access points to exert pressure

For groups with objectives that affect large numbers of people, or that have a national or international impact, access points to decision makers on a local, national and supranational scale are required. In reality, pressure groups are confronted with a wide and growing range of access points — governments and elected officials are increasingly keen to appear consultative. Judging which ones are likely to be the most available and the most effective is the key (see Figure 2).

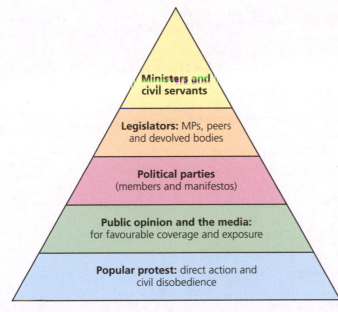

Figure 2 Access points for pressure groups

- Many pressure groups rightly identify ministers and senior civil servants in the **core executive** as the main source of government policy. Groups with insider status are likely to be consulted on government policy if they are sources of valuable and expert information and can provide a reliable and responsible sounding board for government proposals. Groups such as the British Medical Association and the Institute of Directors are consulted frequently by the Department of Health and the Treasury respectively.

- Groups may supplement their inside access by (or be limited to) lobbying MPs and peers within **Parliament**. Many groups submit written evidence to select committees or urge supportive MPs to introduce Private Members' Bills.

- Devolution has brought new tiers of decision making to a **regional level**. For example, ASH Scotland was successful in banning smoking in public places in Scotland a year before the rest of the UK. Additionally, elected mayors have brought greater power to cities — ukfeminista lobbied the London mayor's office to make public transport in the capital safer for women.

- The dominance of parties within the UK's parliamentary system means that it is sensible for groups to aim to influence **party policy**. Many groups contribute to party funds — especially trades unions and the Labour Party — and shaping party policy in the form of manifesto commitments is a key way for many pressure groups to achieve success.

■ Influencing the government indirectly by demonstrating wide **public support** for a cause is a classic attention-grabbing tactic. Protests and demonstrations can worry governments, and coordinated campaigns to raise awareness through well-known **media** channels can ensure that officials incorporate ideas within policies, even if this is not admitted openly.

■ **Direct action** is time-honoured tactic that, in the age of rapid communication, has become a much more popular and mainstream way of exerting pressure. Whether through court cases, civil disobedience, flash mobs, publicity stunts, trending hashtags or conventional demonstrations, many pressure groups use some form of direct action tactics.

> **Exam tip**
>
> Ensure that you use some of the very latest examples of direct action to support your arguments.

Factors likely to affect the political influence of different groups

Measures of success vary enormously from one pressure group to another. For some, success is very specific (e.g. ASH and legislation to ban smoking in public places), for others the campaign is ongoing (e.g. Heathrow No Third Runway Action Group), for others still, success revolves around raising constant awareness (e.g. Passive Pressure UK representing animal welfare issues). However, there are some clearly identifiable factors which affect chances of success:

■ **Aims and philosophy** — if goals are achievable and decision makers are sympathetic.

■ **Status** — while there are no guarantees that insider groups will enjoy more success than outsiders, access to decision makers is clearly beneficial.

■ **Expertise** — credible, specialist knowledge can be vital to government decision making.

■ **Wealth** — money can fund extensive campaigns and 'buy influence' with political parties.

■ **Size** — groups with large numbers of potential voters are difficult to ignore.

■ **Organisation and leadership** — effective and coordinated media and public awareness campaigns.

■ **Other factors** — celebrity endorsement, the presence of opposition groups and the timing of issues can all play a part in achieving success.

For many pressure groups operating in the complex and uncertain world of the UK's fragmented democracy, the quality, commitment and determination of staff is the single biggest factor in determining success. Innovative and committed leadership is a prerequisite. Well-resourced groups can attract highly qualified and effective staff, recruited directly from the country's best universities. With a collective understanding of the group's strategy and the ability to use new technology to build engagement and support, groups can rise rapidly to disrupt the status quo and achieve success. Expert and engaged staff — along with an alignment with the sympathies of the government — are the common factor in the following successful groups:

■ In the 1990s a little-known group called Liberty began its rise to significance through strong connections with the Labour leadership. The group succeeded notably in pushing human rights legislation to the top of the political agenda.

- In the 2000s, Policy Exchange (created in 2002) was regarded as the then prime minister David Cameron's 'favourite think tank', influencing ministers, academics and journalists alike.
- In the 2010s the Centre for Social Justice (CSJ) and Reform — two leading pressure groups campaigning for public service reform and social responsibility — are at the centre of government social and economic policy formulation.

Links with political parties

How do pressure groups differ from political parties?

The blurring of the traditional distinction between pressure groups and parties is a significant recent feature in the UK. Pressure groups and political parties both seek to educate the public about significant issues, often providing opposing perspectives that formulate different opinions. However, pressure groups are usually only formed for one reason (e.g. Surfers Against Sewage campaigns for cleaner seas around the UK) and may be short term (like many cause groups), whereas parties are multi-issued, tend to last a long period of time and attempt to appeal to as wide a range of potential voters as possible.

Perhaps the traditional distinction of pressure groups not being parties because they do not develop a 'range of policies' is not as appropriate as it used to be since many well-organised pressure groups hold meetings, canvass for votes and distribute leaflets — just like political parties do. A key difference may be that the machinery to 'win votes' where pressure groups are concerned is only cranked up prior to an election — making electioneering only a small feature of their wider activities. For parties however, this machinery is permanent and continuous over the long term — usually at all (or many) levels: local, regional, national and European.

How do pressure groups work through political parties?

Some pressure groups are recognised as being close to one of the main parties — for example, the Confederation of British Industry has been known to work closely with the Conservatives, while the trade unions are historically linked to the Labour Party. This kind of close association can ensure that the group has a hand (or at least is consulted) when policies are being shaped. Prior to elections, the most successful groups are able to get their issues onto the various parties' manifestos.

Exam tip

Ensure that you can illustrate your answers with specific examples of how the boundaries between pressure groups and parties have become blurred.

Summary

After studying this topic you should be able to:
- Define the term pressure group and ensure that the nature of pressure groups' activity within modern democratic states is well understood.
- Evaluate and explain the various typologies of pressure group activity — sectional and cause, insider and outsider.
- Analyse and group the factors that influence pressure group success — using contemporary examples to exemplify why some groups are more successful than others.
- Demonstrate an awareness of the methods that pressure groups employ, especially where the pressure is directed and how access points might have changed.
- Understand the differences between political parties and pressure groups, and the relationships between them.

■ The European Union

The UK's relationship with the European Union (EU) has been a complex and controversial one. Its membership of the EU has had an impact on all aspects of the UK's politics and public policy. It has undermined long-standing constitutional principles and divided parties and public opinion. For some, the freedom of movement and trade and the settled relationships that exist between the member states is a price worth paying for the expensive bureaucracies of the EU's supranational institutions. However, debate over the advantages and disadvantages of the UK's membership was rendered obsolete in June 2016 when a narrow referendum victory for 'Leave' began the process of the UK leaving the European Union.

EU institutions

The EU and its institutions: development

The EU has its origins in the European Coal and Steel Community formed in 1952 between France, Germany and Italy. In the following decades it steadily expanded its membership and responsibilities until the UK joined the European Economic Community in January 1973. Some notable milestones in the development of the EU are outlined in Table 11.

Table 11 Notable milestones in the development of the EU and its institutions

Selected milestones	Year	Significance
Single European Act	1986	The establishment of an internal market within the EU, allowing free movement of goods and workers. Introduction of qualified majority voting (QMV).
Maastricht Treaty	1992	Expansion of the free movement of goods, services and EU nationals — leading to a new sense of European 'citizenship' and laying the foundations for joint foreign and security policies.
Treaty of Amsterdam	1997	Codified the EU Social Chapter, concentrating on human rights and freedoms, although the UK had an opt out under John Major.
Treaty of Nice	2001	Enlargement and consolidation of existing institutions. European Commission to have one member per state, broadening QMV.
Enlargement to 25 member states	2004	Ten states became members in 2004 (including former Soviet satellite states) to transform the breadth and size of the EU.
European Constitution	2004	Restructuring to acknowledge expansion of EU — strengthening the role of European Parliament — SUSPENDED.
Lisbon Treaty	2007	Redrafted 'constitution' with the UK securing opt outs over justice and home affairs.

The EU and its institutions: functions

The European Commission

The European Commission is the 'executive' of the EU, made up of 28 commissioners (one from each state) and a president. It proposes legislation and attempts to ensure that the provisions of the various treaties are upheld. Commissioners are expected to adopt a **supranational** attitude. The Commission has the role of initiating legislation and making proposals to the Council and the European Parliament. It also acts as the guardian of EU treaties and holds power to *execute* agreed policies.

The Council (of Ministers)

The Council is made up of ministers of the 28 member states — the actual minister attending meetings depends on the nature of the issue being discussed. It is the main decision-making body of the EU. While a small number of key decisions are reached by unanimous vote, most are taken on the basis of **qualified majority voting**.

The European Council

The European Council is the forum for heads of state, foreign secretaries and commissioners to determine the direction of the EU. While the European Council has no formal legislative power, its responsibility is to define 'the general political directions and priorities' of the EU. It is referred to as the EU's strategic (and crisis solving) body, acting as the collective presidency of the EU. The Council of Ministers and the European Council are **intergovernmental** bodies.

The European Parliament

The European Parliament is made up of 751 MEPs elected from member states every 5 years. Its primary roles are to scrutinise the EU budget and the European Commission itself. The European Parliament is the only EU institution that is democratically elected by citizens in each member state. Seats are allocated to individual states in broad proportion to population. Once only advisory, the modern European Parliament has legislative powers over certain areas (e.g. the environment) under the so-called co-decision procedure. The European Parliament approves the EU budget and confirms the Commission's appointment. Parliamentary censure of the Commission forces its resignation.

The European Court of Justice (ECJ)

The ECJ administers and adjudicates on EU law. Made up of 28 judges (one from each member state) it is able to strike down domestic laws where they conflict with EU law.

The EU and its institutions: where does power lie?

Under the Treaty of Rome (1957) most power within the EEC was vested in institutions such as the Commission and the Council of Ministers, rather than the European Parliament. As the European Parliament remains the only directly elected EU institution, those on the left have argued that it possesses a better mandate to legislate than the Council of Ministers, whose members are normally elected politicians in their own countries but are not directly elected to the Council of Ministers, or the Commission whose members are political appointees.

Supranationalism Cooperation between governments and their appointees at a level that ignores national interests. The EU **Commission**, the European **Parliament** and the **Court of Justice** are supranational bodies.

Qualified majority voting (QMV) A system of weighted voting that contrasts with decisions requiring unanimity. QMV gives member states votes in the Council according to population and size (e.g. Germany has more than three times the number of votes as Finland).

Intergovernmentalism Cooperation between governments of EU member states without abandoning national interests.

The transfer of legislative and policy-making areas from national bodies (elected and accountable to their national electorates) to EU institutions (far less accountable to national voters) has resulted in a decline in traditional and expected levels of checks and balances and an erosion of authority. The complex workings of the EU and its secretive decision making and negotiation practices add to this. Turnout in the UK for the European Parliament elections in 2014 was just 36%.

In order to address the EU's 'democratic deficit':

- The Lisbon Treaty extended the power of the European Parliament.
- Decision making within the Council of Ministers was to become more open and public.
- A new secession clause explains how states can leave the EU.

Debate: does the EU suffer from a democratic deficit

Yes, the EU suffers from a '**democratic deficit**':

- The power to make policy lies with unelected EU institutions such as the Council rather than the elected European Parliament.
- The only elected and accountable institution — the European Parliament — is weak and marginal.
- Too little is known and understood about political activity at EU level or about the performance of elected representatives.

No, claims of a 'democratic deficit' are exaggerated:

- Both the Council (of Ministers) and the European Council (or Summit) are made up of officials who are accountable to their own electorates.
- All key treaties are ratified by member states through representative assemblies or by referendum.
- The role and status of the European Parliament is steadily growing in significance.

Aims of the EU and the extent to which these have been achieved

Aims of the EU

In Article 3 of the EU treaty the main aims of the European Union are set out. Its aims were primarily economic and social and also connected to combating discrimination and promoting EU values of justice, peace and stability.

The creation of a single European market, or internal market in which the free movement of goods, services, persons and capital is ensured was the central and overriding aim of the European Union. The 'four freedoms' to establish this involve:

- the free movement of goods — meaning that member states cannot impose duties or taxes on goods from another EU state, or directly discriminate against them
- the free movement of services — enabling professionals, businesses and self-employed people to offer their services across the EU

Democratic deficit
Referring to power being removed from elected institutions and placed in the hands of those not directly accountable to the people.

Knowledge check 28

Identify two arguments in support of the argument that the EU suffers from a democratic deficit.

Exam tip

Use data from recent European elections — in the UK and in the rest of Europe — to illustrate potential disillusionment with European democracy.

- the free movement of people — allowing any national of an EU member state to seek employment in another EU state without discrimination on the grounds of their nationality
- the free movement of capital — restrictions on capital movements between EU member states (e.g. on buying currency and foreign investment) have been removed.

Achievement of its aims

While the single European market is widely regarded as one of the EU's successes (it is estimated to have created more than 2.5 million jobs across the EU and helped to increase GDP by 15%), some sectors (e.g. energy and public procurement) have proved difficult to open up. Critics in the UK note that EU regulations are costly for small and medium-sized enterprises, and financial services. In this regard, EU policy has also been seen as imposing costs on successful businesses in order to distribute wealth to less competitive businesses in poorer regions.

The free movement of people — a core principle of the EU — has proved to be far more burdensome for some EU countries than others. Eastward migration has meant that destabilising demographic and skills gaps have occurred in states such as Poland, Latvia and Lithuania. In contrast, by 2015 3.2 million EU citizens were living in the UK, representing over 5% of its population while 1.2 million UK citizens lived in the rest of the EU. The picture is a complex one: while the net migration figure into the UK was over 160,000 by 2015, well over 80% of working-age EU nationals were in work in the UK.

The abolition of national currencies in many EU countries was hailed as the greatest single achievement of the process of integration and stability. By 2016, 19 of the EU's 28 states had joined the **European Monetary Union** (EMU), overseen by the European Central Bank's monetary policy. While EMU has brought a number of benefits — especially an end to exchange rate uncertainty — the drawback of a loss of national control of currency has been seen as the cause of debt crises and has required ECB bailouts in several members states.

In the area of rights, EU citizenship has furnished members with a range of economic and social rights. EU citizens have rights to vote in European Parliament elections and local elections, to move to another member state in order to work or reside and the right to permanent residence in another EU country if they have lived there legally for 5 years. Discrimination against EU citizens on the grounds of their nationality is prohibited. In addition, EU law has also extended workers' rights by limiting working hours, improving health and safety and prohibiting discrimination in the workplace.

The EU Charter of Fundamental Rights was a legally binding element of the Lisbon Treaty. The charter served to entrench rights enshrined in the European Convention on Human Rights. These cover dignity (e.g. right to life), freedoms (e.g. liberty), equality (e.g. prohibition of discrimination), solidarity (e.g. workers' rights) and citizen's rights (e.g. free movement). For many people, the EU's aims of combating discrimination and promoting social equality have been its biggest achievements.

European Monetary Union The roadmap towards the creation of a single European currency (the euro) involving convergence criteria for any potential joiner.

Knowledge check 29

Outline and explain the relevance of the European Court of Human Rights.

Exam tip

Provide specific examples of how the EU's promotion of rights has enhanced the lives of previously marginalised groups.

The impact of the EU on UK politics and policymaking

Debate: has the EU eroded UK sovereignty?

What is sovereignty?

National sovereignty refers to the idea that final, supreme decision-making authority is located within the nation state, with the national government determining law for its own territory.

It is useful to separate legal sovereignty from political sovereignty. Legal sovereignty refers to ultimate decision-making authority *in theory*. Critics of the 'European project' have targeted the loss of power over national law in key areas of policy as being the biggest single reason for the UK to leave the EU. On the other hand, political sovereignty concerns the ability to genuinely exercise that 'supreme' power. Supporters of the UK's membership of the EU maintain that the harsh reality of globalisation and the dominance of multinational companies and international agencies mean that the UK's ability to be 'sovereign' is severely restricted. The supportive arguments of EU membership stress that on joining the EU, the UK shared its sovereignty with other EU states in order to increase its influence and capacity to act.

Has EU membership eroded UK sovereignty?

There is no doubt that EU membership severely challenged UK sovereignty. Under the European Communities Act 1972 EU law has primacy in cases where national and EU law conflict. The 1990 *Factortame* case demonstrated this when the UK Merchant Shipping Act 1988, which had restricted non-British citizens from registering boats as British in order to qualify for the UK's quota under the Common Fisheries Policy, was set aside or 'disapplied' on account of its conflict with EU law.

The fundamental constitutional principle upon which the UK is based — parliamentary sovereignty — was therefore demonstrably undermined. However, Parliament always retained ultimate legislative authority as it could repeal the European Communities Act, for which the 2016 referendum result provided the basis.

Was Parliament sovereign anyway?

However, it is important to note that European membership is just one of many factors in the erosion of parliamentary sovereignty that has occurred in recent years. The steady accumulation of power in the hands of the executive has often rendered Parliament ineffective, especially in times of weak opposition and healthy government majorities — the rise of disciplined parties has rendered traditional understandings of legislature-executive relationships outdated. In addition, the use of referendums, the delegation of responsibility for complex legislation to non-parliamentary bodies, the rise of unaccountable and unelected quangos and the devolution of power to the regions make the debate that it is the EU that has eroded parliamentary sovereignty look inaccurate.

Will Brexit restore national sovereignty?

In a technical sense, following its exit the UK will no longer have another authority — at least in the form of the EU — able to strike down national laws where conflicts

Parliamentary sovereignty The principle that ultimate authority resides with Parliament, which is the supreme law-making body.

Knowledge check 30

Outline two arguments that were prominent in the Leave campaign's drive to exit the EU.

arise. In addition, key areas of policy — agriculture, health and safety, environmental protection — will return to the jurisdiction of the UK Parliament. However, in other senses, the extent to which any state can act independently is moot, in an era of globalisation and the pooled sovereignty that the UK enjoyed to determine EU policy and direction will be gone.

In assessing the erosion of national sovereignty that has occurred, an understanding of the constitutional principle of parliamentary sovereignty and the impact of specific European legislation which has bound the UK to the EU — especially the Treaty of Rome (1957), the European Communities Act (1972), the Single European Act (1986) and the Lisbon Treaty (2007) is needed. It also requires an understanding of the changing relationship between UK domestic law and EU law.

Exam tip

Be clear about the areas of policy competence that will be returned to the UK on its exit from the EU.

Summary

After studying this topic you should be able to:
- Understand the working of the EU and its institutions.
- Analyse the decision-making powers of the EU and where decision making lies.
- Evaluate the EU's core aims and the extent to which these core aims have been met.
- Analyse the impact of the EU on UK policy making and, in particular, the extent to which parliamentary sovereignty has been eroded by EU membership.

Questions & Answers

How to use this section

As is the case with any other study aid, this book is aimed at helping you develop your work — it does not do the work for you. The best way to use this section of the guide is to look at each question and make notes on how you would go about answering it, including the key facts and knowledge you would use, the relevant examples, the analysis, arguments and evaluations you would deploy and the conclusions you would reach. You should also make a plan of how you would answer the whole question, taking account of the tips (indicated by the icon **e**) immediately below the question.

After each specimen question there is an exemplar answer. The commentary (indicated by the icon **e** that follows it) points out the answer's strengths and weaknesses. You should compare the sample answer with your own notes and amend your own notes if necessary. Having done all this, you can then attempt a full answer to the question, aiming to avoid the weaknesses but including the strengths that have been indicated in the specimen answer and explanation of the marks.

Remember that these student answers are *not* model answers for you to learn and reproduce word for word in the examination. It is unlikely that the questions in the examination will be worded exactly as they are here and, in any case, there is always more than one way of answering any question. Remember too that this section covers questions that relate to the Politics of the UK section of the specification. Other topics and sample answers are covered in the *Government of the UK* guide.

Assessment objectives

The assessment objectives applied at AS and A-level are:

- **AO1:** Demonstrate knowledge and understanding of political institutions, processes, concepts, theories and issues.
- **AO2:** Analyse aspects of politics and political information, including in relation to parallels, connections, similarities and differences.
- **AO3:** Evaluate aspects of politics and political information, including to construct arguments, make substantiated judgements and draw conclusions.

The AS examination (one paper)

Title: *Government and Politics of the UK*

Duration: 3 hours

Total marks available: 98

Weighting: 100% of the AS

Aim to spend approximately:
- 11 minutes on each 6-mark question
- 25 minutes on each 12-mark extract-based question
- 40 minutes on each 25-mark essay question

The A-level examination (Paper 1)

Title: *Government and Politics of the UK*

Duration: 2 hours

Total marks available: 77

Weighting: $33\frac{1}{3}\%$ of the A-level

Aim to spend approximately:
- 14 minutes on each 9-mark question
- 40 minutes on the 25-mark extract-based essay question
- 40 minutes on the 25-mark essay question

■ 6-mark questions (AS only)

There are four of these questions on the AS paper which are assessed using AO1 only.

What do you need to do?

- Provide a clear and accurate definition of the concept, term or phrase identified in the question.
- Develop your explanation and demonstrate your deeper understanding by selecting and using appropriate examples in support of your answer.

Democracy and participation

> Explain, with examples, the concept of direct democracy. **(6 marks)**

🅮 You should ensure that you have provided a clear and accurate definition of the term direct democracy, along with supporting examples that demonstrate what this means in practice. High-level responses will also demonstrate conceptual understanding of the difference between direct democracy and representative democracy and be able to provide examples from states other than the UK (e.g. Switzerland and the USA).

Student answer

Direct democracy is a process of decision making whereby the people make important political and constitutional decisions, not their representatives. The term originated in ancient Athens when citizens of the city-state (which only included free men) had the opportunity to debate and vote on policy. The practical considerations of mass participation in multiple decisions mean that direct democracy is not possible in modern democratic states and the UK is principally a representative democracy in which elections are used to transfer the responsibility for voting and debating to elected officials. 🅐 However, there are some states that do use direct democracy frequently. Switzerland has around a dozen direct decision-making opportunities each year on a whole range of civic matters, and California sees multiple questions on the ballot — from outlawing capital punishment to legalising marihuana. 🅑 In the UK, opportunities for direct decision making on the part of the people are far less frequent. In fact, up until 20 years ago, they were considered (by Clement Attlee) to be 'alien to our traditions'. Since 1997 however some of the most significant constitutional changes have been determined by popular referendum — from the creation of devolved assemblies in Scotland and Wales (1997) to retaining the Westminster electoral system (2011) to Scotland saying 'No' to independence (2014) and the decision to leave the EU (2016). 🅒

🅮 **6/6 marks awarded (Level 3).** 🅐 This answer provides a clear definition with a brief comparison to representative democracy. 🅑 Although the examples could focus on the UK prior to other areas of the world first, 🅒 the range and scope of the student's response is very strong.

Elections and referendums

> **Explain, with examples, the first-past-the-post electoral system used for Westminster elections.** (6 marks)

(e) You should ensure that you have provided a clear and accurate definition of FPTP, along with supporting examples of how the system has worked in the recent past. High-level responses will also demonstrate conceptual understanding of the nature and purpose of elections in the context of wider concepts covered in the course such as representation, participation and legitimacy.

Student answer

First past the post is the electoral system used for electing MPs to Westminster in general elections. It is a majoritarian system known as 'simple plurality' as the constituency winner need only get one more vote than his or her nearest opponent — rather than an absolute majority of 50% of the votes — to win the seat. **a** Under FPTP, voters are given a single vote which is not transferable. Votes are then counted, with the candidate securing the largest number of votes winning. In the UK, FPTP normally operates on the basis of single-member constituencies, that is, where one individual is elected to represent one geographical area. **b** In the June 2017 general election there were 650 such single-member constituencies. The Conservative Party gained the most seats (318 seats — or 49% of the 650) on the back of national support of 42.4% of the vote. **c**

(e) **5/6 marks awarded (Level 3). a** This answer provides a clear definition using good conceptual knowledge, and **b** combines this with some strong vocabulary and wider knowledge of the FPTP system. **c** There are also some effective examples in the form of data from the most recent election. The student could have provided more detail for the defining feature of the FPTP system — its lack of fair translation of votes to seats.

■9-mark questions (A-level only)

There are three of these questions on A-level Paper 1, which are assessed using AO1 (6 marks) and AO2 (3 marks).

What do you need to do?

■ Offer detailed knowledge, explanation and analysis of three distinct things as identified in the question.

■ Support your answer with appropriate examples drawn from your own knowledge.

■ Demonstrate a sound knowledge and understanding of relevant concepts, institutions and processes.

■ Use political vocabulary accurately and appropriately.

Political parties

> **Explain and analyse three arguments in opposition to the view that political parties should be funded by the state.** (9 marks)

ⓔ Level 3 responses will demonstrate a detailed knowledge of relevant political concepts related to the roles of political parties and the extent to which these should be funded by the state. The highest responses will analyse three clear points within a coherent well-exemplified answer.

Student answer

Political parties play a vital role in the democratic process, at their own considerable expense. But efforts to prohibit individuals from contributing to them, focusing on crude arguments about the levelling impact that state funding might have, are simplistic and impractical. a

First, the Political Parties, Elections and Referendums Act 2000 responded to the growing unease that the decline of broad party memberships allowed wealthy organisations and individuals to wield excessive influence. A raft of measures which included the requirement for parties to disclose donations of £5,000 nationally and £1,000 locally and outlawing overseas donations, addressed many of the concerns and subsequent Acts in 2006 and 2009 further regulated the acceptance of loans. Collectively, the trajectory of ever higher electoral spending has been successfully checked. b

Second, the fundamental right to support and sustain causes and interests that are important to us is one to be valued and protected. Political parties have no less a right to the kind of financial support that charities, faiths and interest groups or social movements routinely enjoy. A system of state funding for political parties, one that denies basic opportunities for supportive individuals to contribute flies in the face of most basic principles of a pluralist liberal democracy. c

A third argument to keep state funding away from political parties is that, if funded by the state, they would lose their independence, becoming just another part of the larger apparatus of the state. They need to remain independent entities — alert to their members and able to offer radical solutions to attract new members and voters.

e **8/9 marks awarded (Level 3).** There may well be a temptation to introduce counter arguments, but the question clearly requires three arguments *in opposition* to the view that political parties should be funded by the state. **a** The first paragraph addresses the question clearly with a well-structured and supported point. **b** There follow some effective points in support of each argument, **c** including some sound theoretical and conceptual knowledge. Further specific examples of groups and individuals funding political parties could have been included.

Pressure groups

> **Explain and analyse three ways in which pressure groups enhance the democratic process.**   **(9 marks)**

e Level 3 responses will demonstrate a detailed knowledge of relevant political concepts related to the functions of pressure groups, with particular regard to their role in the context of pluralist, liberal democracies. There will be a sound theoretical understanding of pressure groups. Such responses will analyse three clear points within a coherent, well-exemplified answer.

Student answer

Pressure groups are collections of like-minded individuals looking to influence decision makers or raise awareness for a cause or section of society. Pressure groups play a number of important roles within society, most of which can be seen within the context of our understanding of democracy. **a**

First, pressure groups represent the interests of individuals or groups to those who govern. They occur naturally as in virtually all our activities there are groups seeking to secure favourable legislation or decisions and to avoid unfavourable ones — from hospital patient groups, to caring for the elderly in our community, to protecting our countryside, to keeping our cities safe, people have a natural desire to unite to protect interests that they feel strongly about. **b**

Second, a passive, disengaged or apathetic citizenry is a threat to democracy. When people do not involve themselves in political activity there is a strong probability that government will become dictatorial and unchallenged. Political activism is therefore important, both to prevent excessive accumulation of power and to ensure that government remains accountable to the people. Well-organised groups have proved able to moderate and channel the excesses of a small number of individuals into controlled and purposeful political engagement.

→

Perhaps the most important democratic function of pressure groups is to ensure that all of us, in small or large groups, are acknowledged and afforded an appropriate degree of protection and support. If this does not occur there is a danger that democracy simply becomes rule by the majority. The nineteenth-century liberal philosopher, John Stuart Mill, referred to the dangers of the tyranny of the majority in this context. Just because 51% of people believe something does not make it right and the impact on less vocal sections of society — children, the unwell and the unemployed for example **c** — needs to be guarded by effectively organised groups. Groups such as Shelter (the homeless) and the Howard League (prisoners) do this to good effect. **d**

e **8/9 marks awarded (Level 3).** **a** The introduction to this response sets the scene very well indeed, and **b** the structure of the response is appropriate for the highest level. The student identifies three distinct ways in which pressure groups can enhance democracy. **c** While there is good *general* use of supporting examples **d** the *specific* examples only come in at the end and could easily have been included in greater numbers throughout the response. Further specific examples of pressure group activities enhancing the democratic process could have been included.

■ 12-mark extract-based questions (AS only)

There are two 12-mark questions on the AS paper, which are assessed using AO1 (2 marks), AO2 (6 marks) and AO3 (4 marks).

What do you need to do?

- Offer developed analysis and evaluation of the two extracts provided, in relation to the question posed.
- Demonstrate an understanding of different perspectives, within an analytical structure.
- Demonstrate a sound knowledge and understanding of relevant concepts, institutions and processes.

The European Union

Read the extracts below and answer the question that follows.

Extract 1

One of the most significant impacts of EU membership under the terms of the Treaty of Rome has been the surrendering of sovereignty in many key policy and legislative areas (e.g. agriculture, health and safety). While the UK could always have withdrawn from the EU, on all practical levels, the theory that Parliament is not bound by any other body is substantially undermined by EU membership. When the UK joined the EEC its activities were confined largely to the economic arena and the UK, as one of nine member states, retained a national veto in most significant areas of policy. Since then, the rapid expansion of the EU and the erosion of the national veto have had profound constitutional consequences that have never been fully acknowledged.

From a newspaper article published in 2017

Extract 2

There is no doubt that EU membership severely challenged UK sovereignty. Under the European Communities Act 1972 EU law has primacy in cases where national and EU law conflict. The 1990 *Factortame* case demonstrated this when the UK Merchant Shipping Act 1988, which had restricted non-British citizens from registering boats as British in order to qualify for the UK's quota under the Common Fisheries Policy, was set aside or 'disapplied' on account of its conflict with EU law. The fundamental constitutional principle upon which the UK is based — parliamentary sovereignty — was therefore demonstrably undermined. However, Parliament always retained ultimate legislative authority as it could repeal the European Communities Act, for which the 2016 referendum result provided the basis.

From a monthly political journal published in 2017

Analyse, evaluate and compare the arguments presented in both of the above extracts in order to reach a conclusion on the extent to which EU membership undermined parliamentary sovereignty in the UK.

(12 marks)

(e) Higher-level responses to this question will identify and evaluate the different perspectives offered in the extracts while answering the central question of the extent to which the UK has surrendered sovereignty to the EU. They will demonstrate accurate knowledge and understanding of the mechanics of EU institutions, as well as the implications of the UK's membership, and the wider discussions surrounding the nature and scope of parliamentary sovereignty.

Student answer

The 2016 referendum result that set in motion the UK's exit from the European Union was one of the most significant political events of the postwar period. Not only did it have immediate practical consequences — it led to the resignation of the then prime minister David Cameron, and also to the 2017 general election which resulted in a hung parliament — but it also had constitutional consequences. The issue that has been raised time and again — and ever since the UK joined the EU in 1972 — is the question of parliamentary sovereignty and the extent to which it has been surrendered to the EU.

Both extracts concur that parliamentary sovereignty has been substantially eroded by EU membership. The first extract relates how this loss of sovereignty has been magnified by the expansion of the EU and the reduction of the national veto. The second extract illustrates this with the legal precedent of the *Factortame* case which saw UK law disapplied. a EU membership has seen the steady transfer of key areas of policy and legislation away from democratically accountable UK institutions (e.g. fisheries and agriculture, environmental matters, health and safety). In addition to this, a well-documented 'democratic deficit' prevents the 'sovereignty of the people' by obscuring lines of accountability following the transferral of policy competences in key areas from the UK to the EU — the institutions of the EU are insufficiently accountable to UK voters. c

However, the second extract points out that the UK can leave the EU at any time by repealing the European Communities Act and following the secession plan contained in the Lisbon Treaty — something that the first extract does not mention. b Added to this, is the fact that the European Parliament has expanded its powers of scrutiny and accountability and seats are allocated in proportion to the population of member states and that the UK has successfully negotiated opt outs on key policy areas over the years (e.g. the Social Chapter under John Major) and is not a member of the European single currency. d

In many ways all countries have experienced a loss of sovereignty with the rise of globalisation and international cooperation. States are no longer independent actors and social and environmental issues cannot be dealt with unilaterally or in isolation. e

e **12/12 marks awarded (Level 4).** **a** This response makes good use of the extracts provided. **b** There is a clear sense of how the extracts differ in content, as well an attempt to put the points raised in each of the extracts into their proper context. **c** The response also demonstrates a secure understanding of the implications of EU membership and **d** makes good use of knowledge and examples to illustrate and explain those points made in the extracts. **e** While the conclusion is not absolutely required, it does further reflect a very strong response.

Elections and referendums

Read the extracts below and answer the question that follows.

Extract 1

The electoral system adopted for European parliamentary elections reflected both the need to please those who demanded electoral reform and the desire to bring the UK into line with every other member of the European Union in accordance with various European agreements. The choice of a party list may well have been to ensure that parties remained in control of the selection of candidates, ensuring that left-wing Labour Party prospective candidates were kept off the lists and right-wing eurosceptic Tories similarly so. However, the introduction of regional lists further distanced MEPs from any real relationship with their constituents and it is seen by many as being responsible for the poor turnouts at all post-1999 elections.

From an academic textbook published in 2015

Extract 2

The experience of the Scottish devolution elections points to significant advantages of the additional member system. In successive elections, the FPTP part of the process led to few or no Conservative seats in the Scottish Parliament, but the regional top-up part of the system has rewarded the Conservatives with a sizeable number of MSPs.

In 2016 the Conservative Party received 31 seats in total — 24 of these were from the regional top-up. With almost the same proportion of the vote in the constituencies (22.0%) as in the regions (22.9%) the redistributive effect of AMS's benefit to the Tories, is evident.

From a monthly political journal published in 2017

Analyse, evaluate and compare the arguments presented in both of the above extracts in order to reach a conclusion on the extent to which alternative electoral systems have improved representation.

(12 marks)

e Higher-level responses to this question will identify and evaluate the different perspectives offered in the extracts while answering the central question of the extent to which alternative electoral systems have improved representation. Implicit within the question is a need to compare results to the strengths and weaknesses of FPTP, as far as is practically possible within the time constraints.

Student answer

The large-scale use of alternative electoral systems has been restricted in the UK to elections for the European Parliament, the Stormont Assembly in Northern Ireland, elections to the Scottish Parliament and the Welsh Assembly and the London mayor. There has been a significant impact in terms of changed patterns of voting and representation.

As the second extract states, the use of the list system in regional top-up elements of the devolved assembly elections has produced a relative success for the Conservatives. **a** Not mentioned in the second extract is the success enjoyed by other parties too and the result in 2016, largely down to the hybrid nature of AMS, saw the SNP benefit, gaining 59 of 73 constituency seats based on just 46.5% of the vote. **c**

The first extract certainly identifies aspects and impacts of the list system used for European parliamentary elections. **a** It appears largely negative in its assessment of the systems though, highlighting the party control offered by the list element and the democratic deficit resulting from huge regional 'constituencies', and the decline in voter turnout.

The first extract could have balanced these disadvantages with a more effective analysis of recent results which were far fairer in terms of allocation of votes to seats: in 2014 UKIP won 24 of the 73 seats based on 26% of the vote: a major breakthrough for a supposed minor party. **c** This contrasts starkly to the performance of UKIP in the 2015 general election when 3.8 million votes translated into just one seat. Had UKIP won its fair share of seats in 2015, then a parliamentary presence of 80 seats (12.7%) may have provided a significant platform from which to build — instead of experiencing a major decline to 1.8% of votes in 2017. **d**

Overall, both extracts agree that alternative electoral systems have altered representation significantly. However, where the first focuses rather negatively on the ill effects of the list system, the second extract outlines some benefits for fairer representation under AMS. **b**

e **11/12 marks awarded (Level 4).** **a** The response uses the extracts well and while both extracts deal with the effects of alternative systems, **b** there is a clear sense of how they differ in content. **c** The response also seeks to put the points raised in each of the extracts into their proper context. **d** The response demonstrates a secure understanding of alternative systems, with good use of wider knowledge and examples to illustrate and explain those points made in the extracts. Direct comparisons of electoral outcomes under FPTP could have been contrasted with those of alternative systems.

■ 25-mark extract-based essay questions (A-level only)

There is one 25-mark question on A-level Paper 1, which is assessed using AO1 (5 marks), AO2 (10 marks) and AO3 (10 marks).

What do you need to do?

■ Demonstrate a developed knowledge and understanding of relevant institutions, processes and concepts.

■ Ensure that your response is clearly organised and analytical in style.

■ Offer a balanced and developed analysis of the extract in which the arguments presented in the extract are properly compared.

■ Evaluate the arguments presented using appropriately selected examples and arrive at a well-substantiated conclusion to the question.

Democracy and participation

Read the extract below and answer the question that follows.

Extract 1

Low turnout is a significant problem as it can profoundly undermine the government's legitimacy and its claim to an electoral mandate. In 2005 the Labour Party's vote share was just 35.2% of a 61.4% turnout meaning that less than 22% of the whole electorate voted for the single-party majority government that was formed in its wake, enjoying a 66 seat majority. For all the wider commentary on the fallout from the 2017 general election, the Conservative Party's vote share of 42.5% — and its haul of 318 seats (49% of the total) means that the minority government enjoys as much popular support as any government since the 1980s.

Aside from this, engagement in the most formal method of participation, that of voting in general elections, remains a serious concern. Some may claim that steadily falling turnout since the 1970s reflects broad satisfaction with things as they are. More likely, and more worryingly, the effects of a polarising electoral system should be seen as a serious concern. With the increasing number of 'safe' seats – those secured prior to any general election contest – the potential for disaffection and powerlessness amongst the wider electorate is disturbing.

From a monthly political journal published in 2017

Analyse, evaluate and compare the arguments in the article over the significance of turnout as an indication of the decline in levels of political participation.

(25 marks)

ⓔ Higher-level responses will draw out key points from the extract, analysing the data on turnout and the implications of its decline within wider explanations of legitimacy and participation. The highest level responses will develop this analysis even further and evaluate turnout alongside other examples and methods of political participation.

Student answer

Using the declining national turnout figure as a central plank in the argument that participation has declined should be treated carefully. The extract is correct to be concerned about the level of turnout, but does not provide an effective explanation that turnout is just one indicator of political participation — and not a particularly sophisticated one at that. **b** Nevertheless, as the main method of electing a representative assembly, and subsequently holding representatives within that assembly to account, voting in general elections – as measured by turnout – has a significance that arguably far outweighs other methods of participation.

To begin with, the national figure for turnout at general elections masks some significant variables. The extract cites two recent elections and associated turnout figures to draw conclusions as to the legitimacy that the subsequent governments had. **a** However, as far as a decline in political participation is concerned, in 2015, 30.7 million valid votes were cast, making the overall turnout across the UK 66.2%. One million more votes were cast than in 2010 and in 2017 turnout was at its highest level since 1997, 20 years previously. At the 2017 general election, an estimated 32.2 million people voted — 1.5 million more than at the previous election — with just three constituencies indicating a decline in turnout since 2015. Whatever the concerns about turnout, recent elections indicate that it is rising, rather than falling.

The extract also attempts to use the national turnout figure to make wider points about the nature of political engagement. It indicates that falling turnout may well not reflect disengagement or participation decline, but instead may be down to vagaries of the electoral system. **a** This point is well made since differential turnout reflects the fact that the turnout figure in any given election is made up of widely varying figures. Some closely fought constituency elections in 2015 saw turnout at over 80% (e.g. Dunbarton East at 81.9%) compared to the national average. The seat with the lowest turnout in 2015 was Manchester Central with just 47% of registered voters voting. The extract provides more context by mentioning the rise of apathy. **b** The decline in turnout at recent general elections is seen by some as reflecting a growing sentiment among non-voters that elections change little. For others, satisfaction with the status quo can also lead to abstention (not casting a vote) — often referred to as 'hapathy'.

Socioeconomic factors play a part too — making the national turnout figure as an indicator of a decline in political participation less helpful. Across the last three general elections, turnout for the lowest income third averaged 55% compared to 70% for the highest income third. Turnout among voters with degree-level qualifications averaged 67%. For those with no educational qualifications the figure was 53%. **c**

A further issue, not mentioned in the extract is the fact that the media can play an important part in bringing issues to the attention of voters and constituency elections with high-profile battles can see higher than average turnout. In 2010, Brighton Pavilions saw a turnout of over 70% and a win for the Green Party's

Caroline Lucas, the party's first Westminster MP. **d** Other factors such as the type of election can be significant too: turnout at European Parliament elections in 2014 was just 35.6%. **d**

Overall, the extract provides detail on turnout and some context as to whether the figure should be used as an indicator of the decline in political participation, the issue is considerably more complex and it is clear that a single figure is of very limited value.

e **21/25 marks awarded (Level 5).** **a** This response makes good use of the extract provided, citing a number of points from it. **b** It also picks up the contrasting arguments and differentiates between the main themes of the extract too. **c** It demonstrates a strong base of own knowledge about the nature of turnout and wider political participation within the context. **d** There are a number of good and specific examples, and the student has developed a fairly sophisticated evaluation of political participation outside the framework of electoral participation, though might have included some specific data and might have briefly reviewed turnout at elections other than general elections.

Political parties

Read the extract below and answer the question that follows.

Extract 2

As astonishing as the political fortunes of the SNP were in 2015, its 56 seats cannot be seen to herald a national change in party politics or voting behaviour. In regional terms Scottish constituencies have become a two-party struggle between Labour and the SNP rather than a true multi-party battleground. The emergence of a clear majority for the Conservatives in May 2015 meant that any impact these 56 MPs could have had on the business of the House of Commons has been insignificant. The lack of SNP representation in the House of Lords is also a serious obstacle to the emergence within the Westminster system of something that might equate to a multi-party system.

However, beneath this superficial analysis lie some deeper truths. The Additional Member System (AMS) used in all regions has allowed voters to elect regional 'top-up' representatives as well as constituency MPs, and has seen the majority of votes (if not seats) in recent elections shared between four parties. Whilst the SNP currently dominates seats, Scottish Parliamentary elections, have resulted in wide-ranging outcomes from coalitions to minority- and majority-party governments involving Labour, the Liberal Democrats and the SNP. Use of AMS for elections to the Welsh Assembly has seen many constituencies result in three- and even four-way races. In elections to the Northern Ireland Assembly, where the highly proportional Single Transferable Vote (STV) is used, preferential voting results in few wasted votes and a greater numbers of parties securing seats. In 2011 a total of seven parties shared the 108 seats.

From a newspaper article published in 2017

Analyse, evaluate and compare the arguments in the above extract over the extent to which the UK could be said to have a multi-party system.

(25 marks)

(e) Higher-level responses to this question will demonstrate effective analysis of the extract and wide-ranging own knowledge — not just limited to the effects of alternate systems but also to parliamentary culture and Westminster politics. The best responses will be able to evaluate arguments of the extract and weave them into a wider response with effective examples and synoptic links.

Student answer

Historically, elections in the United Kingdom have been dominated by the Labour and Conservative parties. In the seven general elections that took place between 1950 and 1970 these two parties polled an average vote share of over 93%, winning all but a tiny handful of seats in the process. Since then the steady rise of 'minor' parties, the creation of regional assemblies and the introduction of alternative electoral systems have seen an end of traditional two-party dominance and the creation of a prospering multi-party system in the United Kingdom.

In addition to this, the extract clearly states the case for multi-party politics, citing the impact of alternative electoral systems in the regions. a The evidence points to the fact that where proportional electoral systems are used, a far higher number of parties win seats and voters are far less constrained by a lack of realistic choice.

In the last two general elections around a third of all votes have gone to parties other than the Conservatives or Labour: 2010 saw a peak of 34.9% of voters supporting parties other than the big two. b Ever-increasing vote shares have seen breakthroughs for so-called 'minor' parties in terms of seats won. While in 2001 the nationalist parties secured just 27 seats between them, in 2015 this figure rose to 80, with the Scottish Nationalist Party (SNP) winning 56 seats alone. b Following the 2015 general election a total of 11 different political parties held seats in the Westminster Parliament.

As the extract reveals, multi-party politics is demonstrably alive and well in the regions. a Even in Westminster, where first past the post reigns supreme, a sustained decline in support for the big two parties has seen seats won by other parties rise from 44 in 1992 to 88 in 2015, making the direction of multi-party travel clear. b

However, the counter argument to this is made clear in the first paragraph of the extract which puts a very different slant on the growth of a credible 'third party' and especially the growth in popularity of 'minor' parties like UKIP and the SNP. a The 2015 general election delivered a profoundly 'old-fashioned' result with politics reverting to a more traditional 'two-party' system.

Following the UK's rejection of the AV electoral system (67.9% of the 42.2% turnout against) in the 2011 referendum, a voting system has been preserved which plays into the hands of large political parties – ones with national rather than regional appeal. In 2017 this essential truth was driven home when the SNP lost more than a third (22) of its 56 2015 seats, and when over 82% of the votes were delivered to the two main UK parties. The Conservative and Labour parties secured 580 of the 650 seats, retrieving 17 seats from all other parties (who shared a combined 70 seats) in the process b. It is difficult to see significant advances being made in this area without reform of the voting system: established supportive party 'heartlands' will continue to across the whole of the UK c.

The ebb and flow of nationalist parties in the regions is only one part of the picture though, as the UK's traditional 'Third Party' have remained a firm feature of electoral politics for many decades. In 1983 the Lib-Dems polled almost a quarter of the national vote, broadly on a par with the Labour Party. In their receipt of barely a tenth of Labour's seats – 23 to Labour's 209 – lies the truth of the matter that the parliamentary stranglehold of the two main parties is so difficult to release. Further examples of Lib-Dem gains (22% of the vote in 2010 but less than 10% of the seats) have not led to a reshaping of party politics and, certainly as far as the Lib-Dems are concerned, the picture looks as unshakeable as ever following the 2017 election c.

Whatever the result of a general election, the inescapable fact is that the House of Commons (and to a lesser extent the House of Lords) is designed primarily for a two-party, confrontational style of political debate. There is only one official opposition party, only one seat opposite the prime minister across the dispatch box and only one confrontation that captures the public's imagination in Parliament. b

While some commentators have predicted that increasingly dealigned voting trends will pave the way for a more European style multi-party system, others suggest that as party allegiance loosens the UK will retain its bipartisan nature but along less-defined lines such as exists in the USA. c Ultimately, the extract is accurate in highlighting the contrast between increasingly sophisticated multiparty voting behaviour alongside the bluntness of the pervading two party dominance in Westminster.

e **21/25 marks awarded (Level 5).** a This answer is both specific with regard to the treatment of the extract and b general in the way that it brings in wider knowledge and examples. Overall it is an impressively wide-ranging and analytical response under exam conditions with some highly developed evaluation. c There are some effective synoptic links, though these might have been developed, alongside some further detail on the fortunes of the UKIP and the Green Party too.

■ 25-mark essay questions (AS and A-level)

These questions appear on both the AS Paper, where you must answer one such question, and A-level Paper 1, where you must answer two.

Which of the assessment objectives (AOs) do they assess?

AO	AS	A-level
AO1	7 marks	5 marks
AO2	10 marks	10 marks
AO3	8 marks	10 marks

What do you need to do?

- Demonstrate a developed knowledge and understanding of relevant institutions, processes and concepts.
- Ensure that your response is clearly organised and analytical in style, arriving at a well-substantiated conclusion to the question posed.
- Offer a balanced and developed analysis of the issue at hand.
- Present and evaluate a range of perspectives on the issue at hand, using appropriately selected examples.

Elections and referendums

> 'Referendums should be used more widely.' Analyse
> and evaluate this statement.   (25 marks)

ⓔ Higher-level responses will provide a strong and well-supported definition of referendums, including examples of their use and contextual awareness of why they have generated controversy. Analysis and evaluation will take account of the advantages and disadvantages of referendums with a concluding statement that might differentiate between when referendums are appropriate and when they may not be.

Student answer

In large and modern democracies, the kind of democracy used in Greek antiquity is unlikely to have any practical place. And yet some of the most significant political events and issues of recent years have been determined by referendums — with all their associated strengths and weaknesses. [a]

A referendum is a vote on a single issue put before the electorate by the government, usually in the form of a question requiring a yes or no response. Referendums are rare in the UK, although they have been used relatively frequently since the 1970s for issues of constitutional importance (such as the devolution referendums in Scotland and Wales in 1997 and the Scottish independence referendum of 2014). There is much debate on their constitutional position as they are a feature of direct democracy at odds with the UK's system of representative democracy. Referendums can take place at local, regional and national levels and the most recent UK-wide referendum came in June 2016, when citizens voted to leave the European Union on a 52/48 split.

Arguably the most significant advantage of referendums — and therefore the reason why they should be used more widely — is that they provide a vehicle for direct political participation and encourage political involvement. **c** As A. V. Dicey said, they 'would bring in men to the ballot box who now hardly vote at all'. Voter turnout in general, local and European elections has been in decline for some time. Some people argue that referendums will help to create the sense of a participatory democracy — giving people real power and influence on important social and political issues such as devolution (e.g. Scotland and Wales in 1997) or over a London mayor, 1998. **b** Associated with this is the notion that referendums provide a valuable educative function — in the 1975 EEC referendum it was regularly commented upon that the UK had never been more informed about a single political issue.

Ultimately, even if the results they throw up are unpalatable for some, referendums are seen by many constitutional experts as a 'first best' form of democracy that should be used whenever possible. For all other occasions, the 'second best' of representative democracy will have to suffice.

However, most issues in government are far too complex for average people to comprehend, bringing them down to a 'yes' or 'no' response is an oversimplification. **c** The decision to leave the EU (June 2016) could well have been boosted by large numbers of people who sought to change the status quo, to pass verdict on a political system that appeared to have forgotten about them — and not based on a considered view of the strengths and weaknesses of EU membership itself.

Referendums exhibit one of the central flaws of democracy — that of the tyranny of the majority. Referendums offer an opportunity for a majority to force their will over a minority in a way that may well be unfair or discriminatory. This is in part why Clement Attlee referred to them as 'the devices of demagogues and dictators' — used to provide an illusion of legitimacy for controversial or heavy-handed decisions.

By forcing people to make a decision one way or another on an issue that may not have been significant for them, referendums can be argued to be very divisive. Where level-headed and respected politicians can unite people in difficult times, referendums split the nation often causing more controversy and upheaval than they solve. In the EU referendum the distinct parts of the UK — London, the north, the regions — can be seen to have voted for different outcomes which confirms to disparate groups that actions taken are not in their best interests.

Ultimately, whether referendums should be used more widely or not depends on the issue and the context. The Public Administration and Constitutional Affairs Committee published its report 'Lessons learned from the EU Referendum' in

→

April 2017 confirming that referendums were a firm part of the UK's political fabric — but that using them to resolve issues of party difference (what it termed 'the bluff call' referendum) was not appropriate. **b** Residents of Edinburgh, Birmingham and Manchester have all been satisfied with referendum-based consultation over the years but there remains long-standing rancour over the result and implications of the EU referendum. **d**

e **21/25 marks awarded (Level 5).** **a** This is a succinct and strong essay that starts well, clearly defines the issues and the debates and **b** provides a sound level of exemplification. **c** There are two distinct sides to the argument which stand up well to scrutiny and **c** the level of analysis is strong throughout. **d** There is also a well-substantiated conclusion. An easily rectifiable weakness is the lack of synoptic links which the essay lends itself to — there were opportunities throughout to compare to initiatives in the USA and referendums in Switzerland as well as to delve a little deeper into the differences between direct and representative democracy.

Democracy and participation

'Electoral participation is still dominated by class.'
Analyse and evaluate this statement. (25 marks)

e Higher-level responses will not only identify the ways in which voting behaviour is still shaped by class, but also analyse and evaluate a variety of other factors — notably long-term factors and the extent to which these have been superseded by both short-term factors and also by more sophisticated voting models to explain them. The best essays will demonstrate a thorough knowledge of theories of dealignment and embourgeoisement and provide up-to-date data and examples in support.

Student answer

In the 1960s, Pulzer concluded that 'class is the basis of British party politics; all else is embellishment and detail'. This time-honoured quote was felt to encapsulate the decades immediately following the Second World War when voting behaviour was characterised not only by a close alignment between class and party but also by a healthy relationship between the two. People were proud of their socioeconomic status and proud to support a party that furthered their cause. During these decades the working class voted Labour and the middle classes Conservative. As such, it was said to be an era of high partisan alignment: people voted for 'the party of their class'. **a**

In recent years, however, the relationship between class and voting has been undermined by significant social and economic changes that have brought into play several new factors that determine voting behaviour. Voting is said to be more volatile, more rational and subject to both long-term factors (e.g. patterns based on region and ethnicity) and short-term factors (e.g. personalities and the state of the economy). In spite of this, class — or socioeconomic status — is still said to play a large part in shaping voting behaviour, so this requires significant attention.

Theories of political socialisation suggest that, depending upon how and where people are brought up, they will identify with a certain party to such an extent that they become heavily aligned to it. The decline in traditional manufacturing industries and the rise of the service sector heralded a process referred to as dealignment. Between 1955 and 1996, employment in the service sector increased, while manufacturing employment fell to just 18%. **b** Psephologists such as Butler and Stokes and Ivor Crewe provided evidence for the decline of the working class, the rise of a 'middle-class' and an increasingly volatile electorate.

Factors such as the privatisation of state-run industries and the extension of share ownership made some members of the working class feel more 'middle class' in a process that became known as embourgeoisement. The Housing Act 1980 allowed long-term council house tenants the 'right to buy' their homes at significant discounts. In the 15 years to 1995, 2.1 million council houses were bought privately, netting the Treasury an estimated £28 billion. The process of privatisation was accompanied by a boom in share-ownership — many people owned a personal stake in Britain's companies for the first time. This led to the birth of a 'new working class' of aspiring voters. This new group of less-state-dependent 'owner-occupiers' was considered more likely to identify with the Conservative Party as Margaret Thatcher's 'working-class Tories'. **c**

The upshot of dealignment was that parties had to respond to the changing nature of the electorate. The Labour Party shifted to the left and reaffirmed its commitment to the unions, state-run industry, the preservation of the manufacturing base and causes such as nuclear disarmament. **c** The Conservative Party shifted to the right and championed deregulated industry, low taxation, low public spending and privatisation. The Alford Index (calculated by subtracting the percentage of non-manual voters voting Labour from the percentage of manual voters voting Labour) went down from 42% in 1964 to only 22% in 1997. Margaret Thatcher succeeded during this period in attracting C2 voters: the 'working-class Tories'.

In the mid-1990s, the Labour Party successfully remodelled itself as the party of 'middle England'. By committing itself to Conservative *tax and spend* policies in the immediate post-election period, the Labour Party reassured many traditionally middle-class voters.

The twin processes of dealignment and embourgeoisement heralded an era in which people began to make more rational choices based on factors such as specific policies or issues, the prevailing values or the ideology of a party, the character or style of the leader, or make judgements on the past performance of the government. But there still remain very strong demographic factors (sometimes known as long-term or primacy factors) that appear to be

→

prominent in understanding voting patterns too: region (e.g. North vs South, rural vs urban), age, gender and ethnicity. Pressure groups or specific business and media interests also began to influence voting behaviour in different and more complex ways.

The above factors suggest that voters are much more *rational* in the way they cast their votes and more likely to create a general assessment of parties based on their track record and what they propose to do, thereby making social class a significant but substantially eroded factor in determining voting behaviour. d

e **21/25 marks awarded (Level 5).** Starting with a strong paragraph which establishes context and sets out the ground rules for the discussion always helps to establish a clear pathway for the discussion ahead. a This introduction performs that task very well indeed. It is vitally important not to get side-tracked into exploring all the other areas of this topic — while there is room for discussion on other factors, the essay is primarily about the significance of class. The essay could be improved by bringing it up to date, especially on the current debates about culture replacing class as a significant determining factor. However, there are b plenty of in-depth examples, c balanced and developed analysis, and d a well-thought through conclusion.

Knowledge check answers

1 According to the Electoral Commission, those ineligible to vote are members of the House of Lords; EU citizens (other than UK, Republic of Ireland, Cyprus and Malta) resident in the UK; anyone other than British, Irish and qualifying Commonwealth citizens; convicted persons detained in pursuance of their sentences; anyone found guilty within the previous 5 years of corrupt or illegal practices in connection with an election.

2 During the First World War women took on many jobs — in manufacturing and agriculture — that were previously considered to be the preserve of men. Some of the work, such as in munitions factories, was highly dangerous and vital to the war effort.

3 Significant social and economic changes — such as many more women joining the workforce — have had a significant impact on 'closing' the gender gap.
The Labour Party has reached beyond its traditional support base (working-class men) to attract more women.

4 The iniquities of the UK's FPTP voting system mean that if certain ethnic groups are heavily concentrated in a small number of geographic areas, while they may well win the corresponding seats, many votes over and above the amount required will be wasted.

5 **For:** prisoners should be allowed to vote so that they remain as connected to the community they are from as possible. Many will be released under conditions that they were prevented from having a 'say' in.
Against: prisoners have not met the basic expectations placed on them so they should forfeit some basic rights too.

6 The 2004 North-East referendum was a good example of the government seeking consultation over its plans to create regional assemblies. It was rejected.
The 1997 devolution referendums in Scotland and Wales were good examples of public support entrenching the creation of institutions that some parties did not support.

7 The national turnout figure hides significant regional variations as well as variations among ages, genders and socioeconomic groups.

8 End the badger cull instead of expanding to new areas — debated in March 2017.
Make it illegal for a company to require women to wear high heels at work — debated in March 2017.

9 In 2015 several notable Liberal Democrat MPs were held to account — Simon Hughes and Vince Cable both lost their seats. In 1997 Neil Hamilton was voted out by his Tatton constituents after being embroiled in the 'Cash for questions' scandal.

10 In 1983 Margaret Thatcher's Conservative Party won a total of 397 seats, with Labour's 209 seat haul putting it a distant second.
In 2001 Tony Blair's Labour Party repeated its 1997 landslide by winning 412 seats compared to the second-placed Conservative Party which secured only 166 seats.

11 An example of a safe Labour seat is Bootle, where in the 2010 general election Labour received 66% of the vote, giving it a 51% majority over the second-placed Liberal Democrats (at 15%). Beaconsfield is a safe Conservative seat; in 2010 the party gathered 61% of the vote there, giving it a 41.5% majority. Voters who live in safe seats are well aware that their votes are highly unlikely to make any difference to the outcome of the election.

12 Candidates from a number of different parties are likely to win and therefore various different elements of a community will be represented.
There is a better voter choice of representatives in who they select or approach for assistance.

13 The lack of concentrated constituency support means that the Conservative Party rarely wins constituency seats under FPTP. However, it does gain votes across the regions and this is enough to gain seats in this aspect of the vote.

14 Rational voting — or rational choice models of voting behaviour — sees voters as rational individuals basing their voting preferences on issues, policies and the performance of parties.

15 Advantage: they are another significant way of informing and engaging the electorate to boost turnout and engagement.
Disadvantage: they are inaccurate and inexact in an era of far greater voter volatility.

16 Referendums allow the people to legitimise a policy decision — their popular support for the creation of an institution effectively entrenches or protects it from change without a further referendum.

17 The main reason was that the Labour Party absorbed almost the entirety of the votes of newly enfranchised working classes while the middle classes coalesced around the Conservative Party, completely marginalising the Liberal Party by the middle of the last century.

18 Cameron was keen to 'detoxify' the 'nasty party' with commitments to a 'Big Society' agenda, social justice and liberal social values.
An environmental agenda was embraced, including the logo 'think green, vote blue'.

19 A 'left-wing' ideology that accepts the need for a free market within a capitalist framework but that seeks to use the state to redistribute wealth to avoid the worst excesses or inequalities of the free market.

20 Representation of members' views; allowing individuals to participate at different levels; recruiting future leaders; formulating policy; providing stable government.

21 A device used by the Labour Party to force constituency Labour parties to create and select from women-only lists of candidates. It reached a peak between 1993 and 1996 and was responsible for many female Labour MPs entering Parliament in 1997.

22 UKIP polled 3.8 million votes in the 2015 general election yet only won one seat. Nevertheless its vote share diminished Labour Party support in many marginal constituencies allowing the Conservatives to win a significantly larger number of seats despite only polling 0.8% more votes.

23 A one-party system sees a single party dominate while all other parties are banned — examples might include Nazi Germany or North Korea.

A dominant party system sees many parties exist freely but only one party holding government power for a prolonged period. In the UK between 1979 and 1992 and then between 1997 and 2010 the size of the Tory, then Labour, majorities led many to conclude that the UK had become a dominant-party system.

24 A quango (quasi-autonomous non-governmental organisation) operates independently of government. Quangos perform important roles in regulation (Ofsted) or advice (QCA) but are not subject to the same scrutiny or accountability as ministers are.

25 Some of the most vulnerable members of society — neglected children, the disabled, the homeless, ex-offenders — are protected by pressure groups. They raise funds and awareness in a way that affected individuals and groups most often could not.

26 Beneficial because lobbyists are often a source of expert information, enhancing government thinking and policy. Problematic if wealthy interests are disproportionately able to influence decision makers.

27 Many groups have some kind of insider track — estimated to be 90% of groups — making a typology that differentiates according to levels of access less helpful.

Outsider groups — in theory having to 'resort' to these tactics — have become more successful and more prominent as opportunities for raising awareness have changed through the internet and social media.

28 From an electoral point of view, the EU is often said to suffer from a democratic deficit because turnout at European parliamentary elections to elect MEPs is routinely below 40%, undermining the legitimacy of the assembly created. In addition, the work of the European Union is little known or understood, meaning that holding MEPs to account for their performance is exceptionally difficult.

29 Under the Human Rights Act, the ECtHR is now the UK's final court of appeal for cases under the European Convention on Human Rights (1950).

30 Arguments of the Leave campaign included the undermining of parliamentary sovereignty in key areas of UK policy such as agriculture and environmental protection, and also the issues associated with the free movement of EU nationals across EU borders.

Index